# THE HANDBOOK OF

BRITISH RAILWAYS

# STEAM MOTIVE POWER DEPOTS

C000224933

## CONTENTS

## VOLUME ONE

# SOUTHERN ENGLAND

PAUL SMITH

PLATFORM 5

This book is dedicated to my wife

SHIRLEY

whose bravery and faith has been an inspiration to us all

Out on one of its innumerable sorties across 'foreign' territory in the mid-60's, ex-LNER A3 Class 4-6-2 No.4472 *FLYING SCOTSMAN* calls in at **BASINGSTOKE (SR) MPD** on September 12th, 1964.     *Sid Nash*

# ACKNOWLEDGEMENTS

In the compilation of a work such as this, information is gleaned from a myriad of sources. Scraps of knowledge form the pieces of a huge jigsaw which, I hope, are all dropped into place and present the reader with a coherent record of British Railways Steam Motive Power Depots. It is here that I wish to place on record my thanks to the principal contributors, all fellow Engine Shed Society members: Chris Bush, George Reeve, Chris Hawkins, John Hooper, Nick Pigott and Roger Griffiths. Steve Dymond helped with demolition dates and site updates and I would particularly like to thank WT (Bill) Stubbs and Sid Nash for their considerable assistance and for allowing me access to their collections of shed photographs. Other photographic contributors are acknowledged in the relevant captions and I would like to extend my thanks to them too.

Proof reading is always a laborious chore and I thank Bob Hadley for his efforts in checking and re-checking the copy.

© CROWN COPYRIGHT
All shed maps are reproduced with the permission of the Controller of the Ordnance Survey.

Published by Platform 5 Publishing Ltd., Lydgate House, Lydgate Lane, Sheffield S10 5FH, England.

Printed by Amadeus Press, 517 Leeds Road, Huddersfield, West Yorkshire, HD2 1YJ. Cover by Bayliss Printing, Turner Road, Wakefield, Notts.

ISBN 0 906579 99-6

THE
HANDBOOK
OF

**BRITISH RAILWAYS**

STEAM MOTIVE POWER DEPOTS

# PREFACE TO THE SERIES

The welding of four great railway companies, London Midland & Scottish, London & North Eastern, Southern and Great Western, in 1948 into the nationalised 'British Railways' saw an amalgamation of resources that today would appear incredulous – 19,134 Route Miles, 54,547 Coaches, 683,285 Freight Vehicles and 20,130 Steam Locomotives.

*20,130 Steam Locomotives!* At a rough estimate they would comfortably stretch, buffer to buffer, over 150 miles.

This series of four volumes deals with the sheds, sub-sheds and stabling points that received "official" status and proliferated to accomodate the fuelling and servicing of such a vast number. The objective of this series is not to present the reader with a comprehensive history of each facility, other books, extensively listed in the Index and Bibliography in *Volume 4*, magnificently fulfil this function, but to quite simply record their existence in a concise manner that the reader will find as a useful reference.

Those early days, the first ten years or so, were, to the observer perhaps, the most romantic, seemingly a mere extension of pre-war times. The scramble for total dieselisation and elimination of the wasteful duplication of resources endowed to the twentieth century was still beyond the horizon. It seemed that the branch line engines still pottered back and forth in near-timeless fashion, the pick-up freight wandering from sidings to sidings, more in the way of a diversion than as a commercial enterprise. In this

period engine sheds, too, only suffered minor casualties, the chance to rationalise the areas which had two or more 'rival' depots was not taken up immediately, indeed none of the medium to large establishments could hope to accomodate all their locomotives. Lack of investment in depot buildings merely compounded the problem and British Railways found itself with many decrepit and dilapidated structures, only a lack of alternatives preventing early closure.

The post-nationalisation politics, chronicled over the years, are of no import to this work, other than in those effects upon the engine shed. The major factor that ensured that steam depots would last well into the 1960's at least was the steam locomotive build policy of the early years of BR. The fragile link between the Gulf States and Britain had been brutally exposed during the war, indeed, oil based fuel was still in very short supply in 1948. The accessibility of coal, beyond the reach of foreign interference must have been a powerful argument in favour of the steam locomotive, regardless of the superior efficiency of the diesel engine. The efficiency of an engine with an empty fuel tank is a very large zero!

By 1951 the 'standard' steam locomotives had begun to appear and the fact that alternative forms of motive power were not given a great deal of consideration undoubtedly influenced the design of new engine sheds. Nowhere was this more apparent than in the scheme for modernising locomotive facilities on Teesside where they had a collection of some absolutely appalling buildings, or lack of them, utilised as engine sheds. Thornaby MPD, completed in 1958 (see *Volume 3*) was designed in 1953 purely as a steam depot and was modified to take diesels only in the light

**HELSTON MPD** *(Alec Swain)*

of the 1955 Modernisation Plan. The retention of a roundhouse clearly indicated the continued inclination towards steam locomotion, even at this late stage.

During the heyday of steam on British Railways many sheds received some sort of renewal, mainly of roofs which suffered considerably from the continual blast of grime and chemicals from the inside and the ravages of the weather on the outside.Some of the major depots even received a total rebuild. Ipswich was a case in point, being totally rebuilt in 1954 and a candidate for early total dieselisation as early as 1960. Ironically, this shed, one of the first depots converted to diesels found itself redundant in 1968 and virtually lasted no longer than depots in the north west that serviced steam locomotives into the twilight of the age. The demise of the steam motive power depots, as would be expected, mirrored the fall from grace of the locomotive, closures coming slowly at first, almost negligibly for the first ten years, and then accelerating *pêle-mêle*, finally clattering to a halt on August 4th, 1968.

Today in many places, where the railways have come and gone, it is as if they never existed. Whole stretches of railway lost beneath redevelopments. The only clue to their once existence a 'Station Road' or 'Railway Inn'. Yet in other parts they are an indelible contour, a ribbon of cuttings, embankments, bridges and viaducts. An asset to the landscape. Pleasing to the eye. Shed sites are found in every part of the country, redeveloped, unused, dieselised, electrified, even preserved. Many of the shed buildings, themselves, still survive in use as barns, factories, machine shops, business premises, supermarkets etc. Some are still used by BR in some capacity or other.

This series then, hopefully, ties up all the Motive Power Depots and Stabling Points used by BR and provides a lasting record to their existence. As that unsurpassed thoroughbred of all mechanical devices, the steam locomotive, is fondly remembered visits to the sheds, whether in boyhood or manhood are similarly recalled. The atmosphere of a working steam depot is unique. Today is tomorrow's history and each generation has its own memories. I am sure that those of us who shared in the era of steam do not envy any other.

May it evoke many joyful recollections whether as just an observer or as one who spent a working life in the 'Cathedrals of Steam'

PAUL SMITH
Birmingham 1989

# BIBLIOGRAPHY

*The principal sources of reference for this volume were;*
An Historical Survey of Great Western Engine Sheds 1947 by E.Lyons (OPC) SBN 902888 16 1
An Historical Survey of Great Western Engine Sheds 1837-1947 by E.Lyons and E.Mountford (OPC) ISBN 0 86093 019 X
An Historical Survey of Southern Sheds by Chris Hawkins & George Reeve. (OPC) SBN 86093 020 3
LMS Engine Sheds Vols1 (ISBN 0 906867 02 9), 2 (ISBN 0 906867 05 3) and 4 (ISBN 0 906867 20 7) by Chris Hawkins & George Reeve (Wild Swan Publications)
Great Eastern Railway Engine Sheds Parts 1 (ISBN 0 906867 40 1) and 2 (ISBN 0 906867 48 7) by Chris Hawkins and George Reeve (Wild Swan Publications)
The British Locomotive Shed Directory (1947) by A.L.F.Fuller
British Railways Pre-Grouping Atlas and Gazetteer by W.P.Conolly (Railway Publications Ltd)
Complete British Railways Maps and Gazetteer 1825-1985 by C.J.Wignall (OPC)

WATFORD MPD *(Alec Swain)*

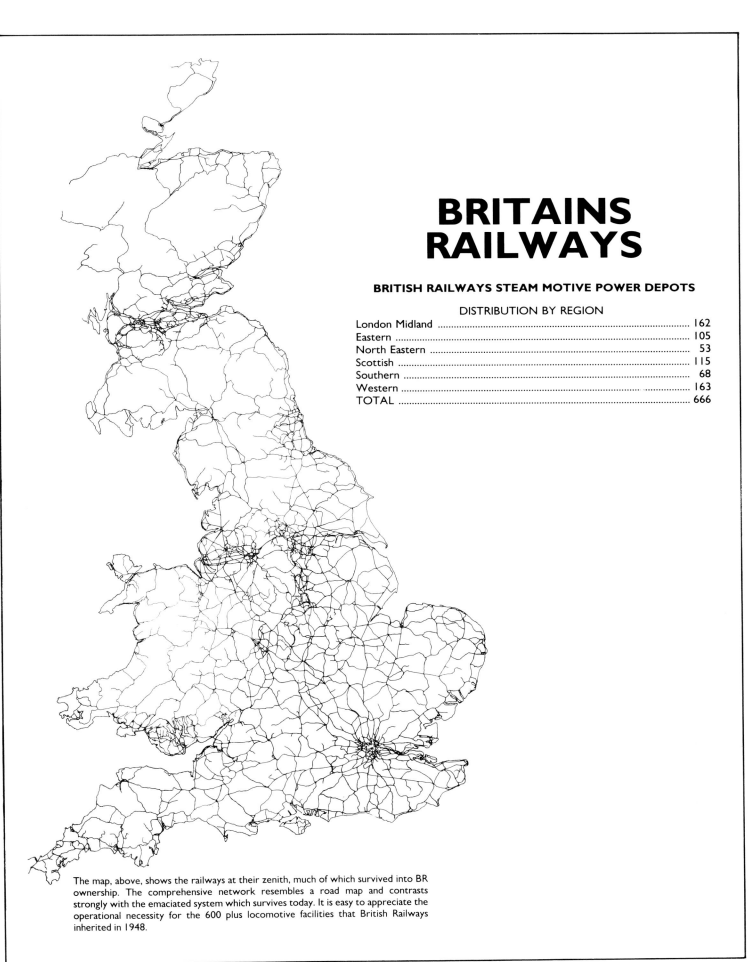

# BRITAINS RAILWAYS

## BRITISH RAILWAYS STEAM MOTIVE POWER DEPOTS

### DISTRIBUTION BY REGION

| | |
|---|---:|
| London Midland | 162 |
| Eastern | 105 |
| North Eastern | 53 |
| Scottish | 115 |
| Southern | 68 |
| Western | 163 |
| TOTAL | 666 |

The map, above, shows the railways at their zenith, much of which survived into BR ownership. The comprehensive network resembles a road map and contrasts strongly with the emaciated system which survives today. It is easy to appreciate the operational necessity for the 600 plus locomotive facilities that British Railways inherited in 1948.

# THE SHED CODES

## BRITISH RAILWAYS

In a perfect world BR would have collated a coded shed list from Day One. The fact that a list did not appear for two years could be partially due to the tremendous re-organisation required to form the railways into 'regions' and not least to the problems involved in overcoming the 'inertia' as old company workings and loyalties remained ingrained.

Fellow Engine Shed Society members, and co-authors of numerous shed books, Messrs Hawkins, Hooper and Reeve have done some research into the early days of BR and I am indebted to them for much of the information reproduced below.

The LMS style of coding was continued as standard British Railways practice, as noted in the Motive Power Committee minutes of June 24th, 1949; "To adopt as standard .... small cast iron plates ... as approved by the Railway Executive 23/06/49" *These being the well known oval-shaped shed plates* . The minutes further continued "Implementation deferred in case of Southern Region ... pending districts being developed and agreed". Hence the adoption of the LMS system and the compilation of a complete shed list, although approved in June 1949 was not able to be expedited until the SR completed its arrangements, which it did on February 27th, 1950.

It is this initial list, *(published by the RCTS in April 1950)* that has been used as the basis for the compilation produced here. Obviously any list of sheds that embraces all from 1948 to 1968 will be crammed with anomalies and as the sheds did not all exist at the same time (eg Shepherds Well closed in 1948, whilst Thornaby did not open until 1958) some liberties have had to be taken to ensure some form of "completeness".

In accumulating this list some 95% of depots automatically, and easily, fall into place in the transition from post grouping to BR. It is the remaining 5% that has caused so much heartache and gnashing of teeth as to when is a shed a shed, or a stabling point a stabling point, and are they of sufficient importance to be included, and not just signing-on points. The reader may well feel aggrieved at the omission or inclusion of a depot. This is not claimed to be the finite, finished article. Just an attempt at sorting out some very grey areas.

Even British Railways found it difficult to tie things up. In 1949 the Motive Power Committee noted that "Often we receive enquiries as to the number of depots which service engines, which are with and without allocations, which have staff, which service and stable and which service only". They further added 'No such list exists' and that they resolved to "get one out". Had this been done, and been published then it could have avoided much debate, and not left later generations to try and sort things out. The humble attempt at resolving this problem is published herewith;

*(For the record British Railways lists on June 3rd, 1949; LMR 137, WR 144, SR 73, ER 95, NER 56, ScR 108. Total number of Motive Power Depots: 613).*

**FARINGDON MPD** *(Alec Swain)*

# LIST OF BRITISH RAILWAYS SHEDS WITH OFFICIAL CODES

(Based upon the first list issued in February 1950, with amendments)

# LONDON MIDLAND REGION

**1A Willesden**
1B Camden
1C Watford
1D Devons Road (Bow)

**2A Rugby**
    Market Harborough
    Seaton
2B Nuneaton
2C Warwick
2D Coventry

**3A Bescot**
3B Bushbury
3C Walsall
3D Aston
3E Monument Lane
    Tipton

**4A Bletchley**
    Cambridge (exLNWR)
    Leighton Buzzard
    Oxford (ex-LMS)
    Newport Pagnell
    Aylesbury
4B Northampton

**5A Crewe North**
    Whitchurch
    Over & Wharton
5B Crewe South
5C Stafford
5D Stoke
5E Alsager
5F Uttoxeter

**6A Chester**
6B Mold Junction
6C Birkenhead
6D Chester Northgate
6E Wrexham
6F Bidston

**7A Llandudno Junction**
7B Bangor
7C Holyhead
7D Rhyl
    Denbigh

**8A Edge Hill**
8B Warrington
    Warrington Arpley
8C Speke Junction
8D Widnes

**9A Longsight**
9B Stockport Edgeley
9C Macclesfield
9D Buxton

**10A Springs Branch**
10B Preston
10C Patricroft
10D Bolton Plodder Lane
10E Sutton Oak

**11A Carnforth**
11B Barrow
    Coniston
11C Oxenholme
11D Tebay

**12A Carlisle Upperby**
12B Carlisle Canal
    Silloth
12C Penrith
12D Workington
12E Moor Row

**13A Trafford Park**
13B Belle Vue
13C Heaton Mersey
    Gowhole
13D Northwich
13E Brunswick Liverpool
    Shore Road (CLC)
    Warrington (CLC)
    Southport (CLC)
    Widnes (GC)
13F Walton
13G Wigan Lower Ince

**14A Cricklewood**
14B Kentish Town
14C St.Albans

**15A Wellingborough**
15B Kettering
15C Leicester
15D Bedford

**16A Nottingham**
    Southwell
    Lincoln (MR)
16B Spital Bridge
16C Kirkby in Ashfield
16D Mansfield

**17A Derby**
17B Burton
    Overseal
    Horninglow
17C Coalville
17D Rowsley
    Cromford
    Middleton Top
    Sheep Pasture

**18A Toton**
18B Westhouses
18C Hasland
    Clay Cross Works
    Morton Colliery
    Williamthorpe Colliery
18D Staveley Barrow Hill
    Sheepbridge Works
    Staveley New Works
    Staveley Old Works

**19A Sheffield Grimesthorpe**
19B Sheffield Millhouses
19C Canklow

**20A Leeds Holbeck**
20B Stourton
20C Royston
20D Normanton
20E Bradford Manningham
    Ilkley

**21A Saltley**
    Camp Hill
    Washwood Heath
    Water Orton

**21B Bournville**
    Redditch
21C Bromsgrove
21D Stratford upon Avon

**22A Bristol Barrow Road**
22B Gloucester Barnwood
    Tewkesbury
    Dursley

**23A Skipton**
    Keighley
23B Hellifield
    Ingleton
23C Lancaster

**24A Accrington**
24B Rose Grove
24C Lostock Hall
24D Lower Darwen

**25A Wakefield**
25B Huddersfield
25C Goole
25D Mirfield
25E Sowerby Bridge
25F Low Moor
25G Farnley Junction

**26A Newton Heath**
26B Agecroft
26C Bolton
    Horwich
26D Bury
26E Bacup
26F Lees Oldham

**27A Bank Hall**
27B Aintree
27C Southport
27D Wigan L&YR

**28A Blackpool Central**
    Blackpool North
28B Fleetwood

# EASTERN REGION

**30A Stratford**
    Brentwood
    Chelmsford
    Epping
    Ongar
    Spitalfields
    Wood St. Walthamstow
    Palace Gates
    Enfield Town
    Ware
30B Hertford East
    Buntingford
30C Bishops Stortford
30D Southend Victoria
    Southminster
    Wickford
30E Colchester
    Clacton
    Walton on Naze
    Kelvedon
    Maldon
    Braintree
30F Parkeston

**31A Cambridge**
    Ely
    Huntingdon East
    Saffron Walden
    Thaxted

31B March
31C Kings Lynn
    Wisbech
    Hunstanton
31D South Lynn
31E Bury St.Edmunds
    Sudbury

**32A Norwich Thorpe**
    Cromer
    Wells on Sea
    Dereham
    Swaffham
    Wymondham
32B Ipswich
    Ipswich Docks
    Laxfield
    Felixstowe Beach
    Aldeburgh
    Framlingham
    Stowmarket
32C Lowestoft
32D Yarmouth South Town
32E Yarmouth Vauxhall
32F Yarmouth Beach
32G Melton Constable
    Norwich City
    Cromer Beach

**33A Plaistow**
    Upminster
33B Tilbury
33C Shoeburyness

**34A Kings Cross**
34B Hornsey
34C Hatfield
34D Hitchin
34E Neasden
    Chesham
    Rickmansworth

**35A New England**
    Spalding
    Bourne
    Stamford
35B Grantham

**36A Doncaster**
36B Mexborough
36C Frodingham
36D Barnsley
36E Retford GN
    Retford GC
    Newark

**37A Leeds Ardsley**
37B Copley Hill
37C Bradford

**38A Colwick**
    Derby Friargate
38B Annesley
    Kirkby Bentinck
    Nottingham Victoria
38C Leicester GC
    Leicester GN
38D Staveley GC
38E Woodford Halse

**39A Gorton**
    Dinting
    Hayfield
    Macclesfield (GC)
39B Sheffield Darnall

**40A Lincoln**
    Lincoln GC
40B Immingham
    New Holland
    Grimsby
40C Louth
40D Tuxford Junction
40E Langwith Junction
40F Boston
    Sleaford

# NORTH EASTERN REGION

**50A York North**
    York LMS
    York South
50B Leeds Neville Hill
50C Selby
50D Starbeck
    Pateley Bridge
50E Scarborough
50F Malton
    Pickering
50G Whitby

**51A Darlington**
    Middleton in Teesdale
51B Newport
51C West Hartlepool
51D Middlesbrough
    Guisborough
51E Stockton
51F West Auckland
    Wearhead
51G Haverton Hill
51H Kirkby Stephen
51J Northallerton
    Leyburn
51K Saltburn
51L Thornaby

**52A Gateshead**
    Bowes Bridge
52B Heaton
52C Blaydon
    Alston
    Hexham
    Reedsmouth
52D Tweedmouth
    Alnmouth
    Duns
    Seahouses
52E Percy Main
52F North Blyth
    South Blyth
    Rothbury

**53A Hull Dairycoates**
53B Hull Botanic Gardens
53C Hull Springhead
    Alexandra Dock
53D Bridlington
53E Cudworth

**54A Sunderland South Dock**
    Durham
54B Tyne Dock
    Pelton Level
54C Borough Gardens
54D Consett

# SCOTTISH REGION

**60A Inverness**
    Dingwall
    Fortrose
    Kyle of Lochalsh
60B Aviemore
    Boat of Garten
60C Helmsdale
    Dornoch
    Tain
60D Wick
    Thurso
60E Forres

**61A Kittybrewster**
    Alford
    Inverurie
    Ballater
    Fraserburgh
    Macduff
    Peterhead
61B Aberdeen Ferryhill
61C Keith
    Banff
    Elgin

**62A Thornton Junction**
    Anstruther
    Burntisland
    Kirkcaldy
    Ladybank
    Methil
62B Dundee Tay Bridge
    Arbroath
    Dundee West
    Montrose
    St.Andrews
    Tayport

**62C Dunfermline Upper**
    Alloa
    Inverkeithing
    Kelty
    Loch Leven

**63A Perth South**
    Aberfeldy
    Alyth
    Blair Atholl
    Crieff
63B Stirling
    Killin Loch Tay
    Stirling Shore Road
63C Forfar
    Brechin
63D Fort William
    Mallaig
63E Oban
    Ballachulish

**64A St.Margarets**
    Dunbar
    Galashiels
    Granton
    Hardengreen
    Longniddry
    North Berwick
    North Leith
    Peebles
    Penicuick
    Polton
    Seafield
    South Leith

**64B Haymarket**
**64C Dalry Road**
**64D Carstairs**
**64E Polmont**
    Kinniel
64F Bathgate
64G Hawick
    Kelso
    Riccarton Junction
    Jedburgh
    St.Boswells

**65A Eastfield**
    Aberfoyle
    Kilsyth
    Lennoxtown
    Whiteinch
65B St.Rollox
65C Parkhead
65D Dawsholm
    Dumbarton
    Stobcross
65E Kipps
65F Grangemouth
65G Yoker
65H Helensburgh
    Arrochar
65I Balloch

**66A Polmadie**
    Paisley St.James
66B Motherwell
    Morningside
66C Hamilton
66D Greenock Ladyburn
    Princes Pier

**67A Corkerhill**
67B Hurlford
    Beith
    Muirkirk
67C Ayr
67D Ardrossan

**68A Carlisle Kingmoor**
    Durran Hill
68B Dumfries
    Kirkcudbright
68C Stranraer
    Newton Stewart
68D Beattock
    Lockerbie

# SOUTHERN REGION

**70A Nine Elms**
70B Feltham
70C Guildford
70D Basingstoke
70E Reading South

**71A Eastleigh**
    Winchester City
    Lymington
    Andover Junction
    Southampton Terminus
71B Bournemouth
    Swanage
    Hamworthy Junction
71C Dorchester
71D Fratton
    Gosport
71E Newport IOW
71F Ryde IOW
71G Bath Green Park
    Branksome
    Radstock
71H Templecombe
71I Southampton Docks
    Southampton New Docks
71J Highbridge
    Wells LMS

**72A Exmouth Junction**
    Seaton
    Lyme Regis
    Exmouth
    Okehampton
    Bude
    Launceston SR
72B Salisbury
72C Yeovil Town
    Templecombe Upper
72D Plymouth Friary
    Callington
72E Barnstaple Junction
    Torrington
    Ilfracombe
72F Wadebridge

**73A Stewarts Lane**
73B Bricklayers Arms
    Ewer Street
    New Cross Gate
73C Hither Green
73D Gillingham
73E Faversham

**74A Ashford**
    Canterbury West
    Margate
    Rolvenden
74B Ramsgate
74C Dover
    Folkestone Junction
    Shepherds Well
74D Tonbridge
74E St.Leonards

**75A Brighton**
    Newhaven
75B Redhill
75C Norwood Junction
75D Horsham
    Bognor
75E Three Bridges
75F Tunbridge Wells West
75G Eastbourne

# WESTERN REGION

**81A Old Oak Common**
81B Slough
      Aylesbury
      Marlow
      Watlington
81C Southall
      Staines
81D Reading GWR
      Basingstoke
      Henley on Thames
81E Didcot
      Lambourn
      Newbury
      Wallingford
      Winchester Chesil
81F Oxford
      Abingdon
      Fairford

**82A Bristol Bath Road**
      Bath Spa
      Wells GWR
      Weston-super-Mare
      Yatton
82B St.Philips Marsh
82C Swindon
      Andover
      Chippenham
      Faringdon
      Malmesbury
82D Westbury
      Frome
      Salisbury
82E Yeovil Pen Mill
82F Weymouth
      Bridport

**83A Newton Abbot**
      Ashburton
      Kingsbridge
      Moretonhampstead
83B Taunton
      Barnstaple
      Bridgwater
      Minehead

83C Exeter
      Tiverton Junction
83D Plymouth Laira
      Plymouth Docks
      Princetown
      Launceston
83E St.Blazey
      Bodmin
      Moorswater
83F Truro
83G Penzance
      Helston
      St.Ives

**84A Stafford Road**
84B Oxley
84C Banbury
84D Leamington Spa
      Alcester
84E Tyseley
      Stratford on Avon
84F Stourbridge Junction
84G Shrewsbury
      Ludlow
      Coalport
      Clee Hill
      Craven Arms
      Knighton
      Builth Road
84H Wellington
      Crewe Gresty Lane
      Much Wenlock
84J Croes Newydd
      Bala
      Trawsfynydd
      Penmaenpool
84K Chester

**85A Worcester**
      Evesham
      Honeybourne
      Kingham
85B Gloucester Horton Road
      Cheltenham
      Brimscombe
      Chalford
      Cirencester
      Lydney
      Tetbury
85C Hereford
      Kington
      Ledbury
      Leominster
      Ross on Wye
85D Kidderminster
      Cleobury Mortimer

**86A Newport Ebbw Junction**
86B Newport Pill
86C Cardiff Canton
86D Llantrisant
86E Severn Tunnel Junction
86F Tondu
      Bridgend
86G Pontypool Road
      Pontrilas
      Branches Fork
86H Aberbeeg
86J Aberdare
86K Abergavenny
      Tredegar

**87A Neath Court Sart**
      Glyn Neath
      Neath N&B
87B Duffryn Yard
      Glyncorrwg
87C Danygraig
87D Swansea East Dock
87E Landore
87F Llanelly
      Burry Port
      Pantyfynnon

**87G Carmarthen**
      Newcastle Emlyn
87H Neyland
      Cardigan
      Milford Haven
      Pembroke Dock
      Whitland
87J Goodwick
87K Swansea Victoria
      Upper Bank
      Gurnos
      Llandovery

**88A Cardiff Cathays**
      Radyr
88B Cardiff East Dock
88C Barry
88D Merthyr
      Dowlais Cae Harris
      Dowlais Central
      Rhymney
88E Abercynon
88F Treherbert
      Ferndale
      Pwllyrhebog

**89A Oswestry**
      Kerry
      Llanfyllin
      Llanidloes
      Moat Lane
      Welshpool
      Welshpool WLLR
89B Brecon
      Builth Wells
89C Machynlleth
      Aberayron
      Aberystwyth
      Aberystwyth VR
      Corris
      Portmadoc
      Pwllheli (BR)
      Pwllheli (GWR)

**BASINGSTOKE MPD** (*WT Stubbs Collection*)

**CAMDEN MPD** *(Photomatic)*

# THE SHEDS
## LISTED BY GEOGRAPHICAL AREA

The country has been divided into 19 Parts and each Part is further sub-divided into Counties and Large Conurbations. These parts and Sub-divisions are purely a convenience, based on pre-war County boundaries and having no pretensions as to pinpointing towns and villages within 'modern' boundaries. BR Regions have been acknowledged, as with regards to the coding of a depot, but each area has been considered as an autonomous unit within which all sheds are dealt with, regardless of origin or operating region. This is designed to present the reader with a complete, concise, rather than fragmented, record of the existence of BR Steam Motive Power Depots within an area.

Each PART is prefaced with a map showing the area covered, indicating all the railway lines built within its boundaries (but not necessarily passing into BR ownership nor, indeed, still extant in 1948) and an index of all the sheds dealt with in that part. Each COUNTY or CONURBATION is prefaced with another map, this time showing the approximate location of each depot relative to the railway network.

Within each sub-division, each FACILITY is identified by name and regional code and LOCATED with reference to nearby stations and lines and pinpointed within about 100 metres by an OS reference. The DIRECTIONS, in the style of Aidan Fuller's famous shed directories, are contemporary to its existence. Of all contentious issues with regard to engine sheds, none is more fraught with pot holes than the CLOSURE DATE. Many of those listed are the 'official' ones, but this is by no means decisive. As far as operational requirements went it could have meant an end of a permanent locomotive allocation or permanent staffing, neither of which would have precluded further use of the depot. Indeed, actually closing the building may have just meant that locomotives were serviced and stabled in the yard. Many of the servicing facilities just dwindled away, there being no, nor needing any, 'official' date. Hence the OUT OF USE, in many case no more than just an intelligent stab in the dark.

The DESCRIPTION is of a brief nature, the abbreviation 'TS' being shorthand for track straighthouse. The POST CLOSURE HISTORY traces the use of the buildings and site following closure to steam.

Each of the depots is indicated on a reproduction of an ORDNANCE SURVEY MAP, most of these maps are at a scale of 1:5000 and dated as near as possible to 1948. The object is to present a permanent record of the location within a large area, so that although the shed may have long gone the site can be located by reference to other features, roads or buildings. Although the intention of these maps is not to specifically provide accurate track diagrams many do, indeed, provide this information. Where diagrams are of a more recent vintage the depot has been superimposed over its original site, in many instances providing a very interesting contrast. Further commentary, clarifying the location of the site within an area, the adjacency of the local road network, and other points of interest have been added.

Finally, many of the depots have been illustrated by means of a PHOTOGRAPH.

An INDEX, at the end of this volume lists the sheds in alphabetical order and gives a page reference. A complete index and Bibliography Section for the whole series can be found at the back of *Volume 4.*

# PART ONE
# SOUTH WEST ENGLAND

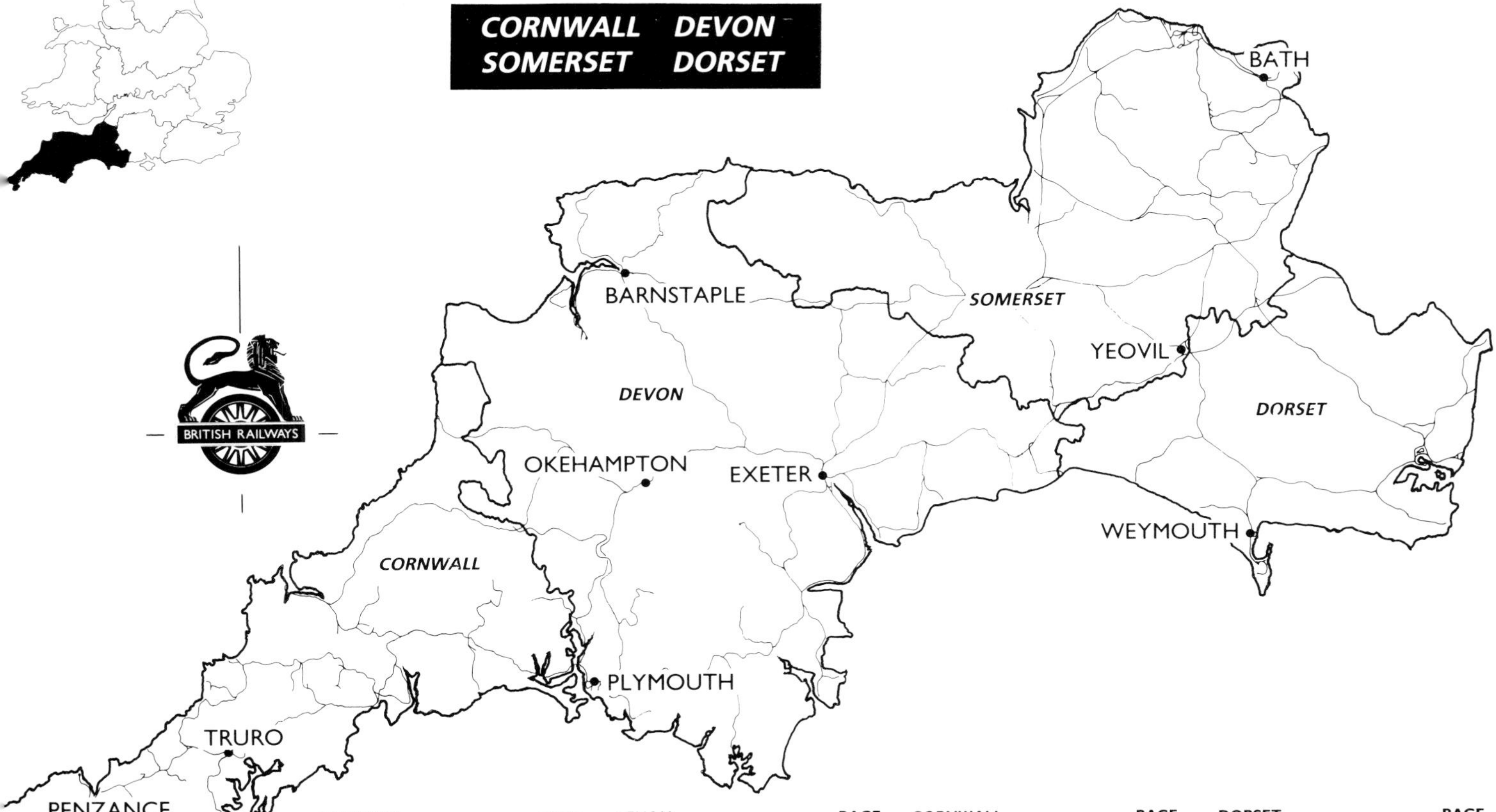

**CORNWALL DEVON**
**SOMERSET DORSET**

BATH

BARNSTAPLE

SOMERSET

YEOVIL

DEVON

DORSET

OKEHAMPTON

EXETER

WEYMOUTH

CORNWALL

PLYMOUTH

TRURO

PENZANCE

BRITISH RAILWAYS

**MORETONHAMPSTEAD MPD** *(Alec Swain)*

# CORNWALL

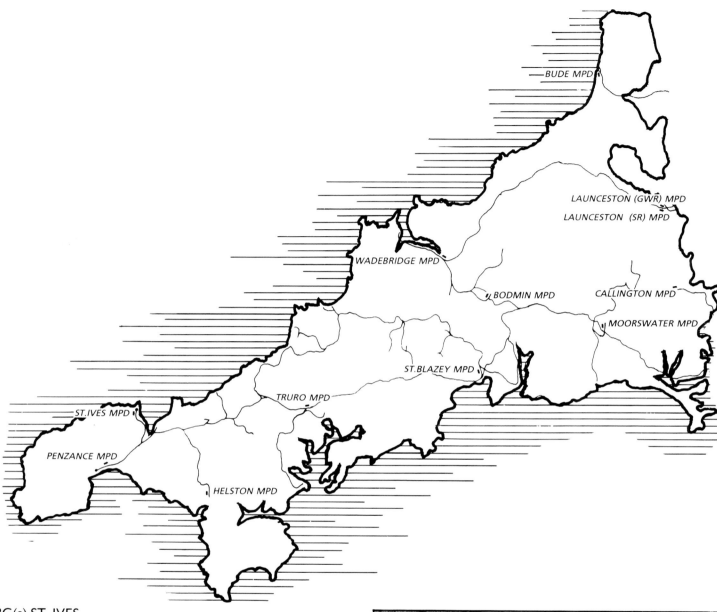

BUDE MPD

LAUNCESTON (GWR) MPD
LAUNCESTON (SR) MPD

WADEBRIDGE MPD

BODMIN MPD

CALLINGTON MPD

MOORSWATER MPD

ST.BLAZEY MPD

TRURO MPD

ST.IVES MPD

PENZANCE MPD

HELSTON MPD

## 83G(s) ST. IVES

**Location**: The shed is west of the line, south of St.Ives Station. (OS Map Ref SW521400)

**Directions**: A pathway leads from the station platforms to the shed.

**Closed**: September 1961.

**Description**: A stone built 1TS dead ended shed.

*Post Closure History*: *Demolished. Site Unused (1988)*

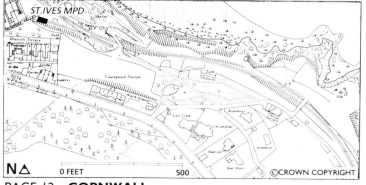

ST.IVES MPD

N△     0 FEET                    500         ©CROWN COPYRIGHT

The shed at **ST.IVES**, photographed on September 26th, 1961 virtually at the point of closure.                                           *WT Stubbs Collection*

**Map Dated**: 1963

## 83F TRURO

**Location**: The shed is north of the line, west of Truro Station. (OS Map Ref; SW813449)

**Directions**: Turn right outside of the station along Station Road, right over the railway bridge and right again into Dobbs Lane. A path leads to the shed from the right hand side of this road

**Closed**: November 1965.

**Description**: A stone built 7TS dead ended shed.

**Post Closure History**: *Demolished. Now site of industrial units. (1988)*

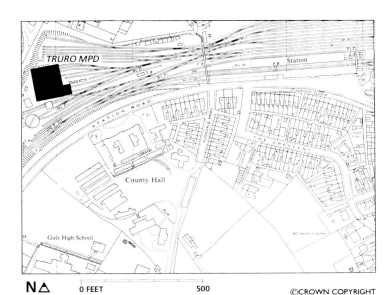

N△    0 FEET    500    ©CROWN COPYRIGHT

**Map Dated**: 1967
**Site Location**: In the west of the town, north of Treyew Road (A390).
**Track Status**: Truro Station and lines are operational.

**TRURO MPD** viewed from the footbridge at the western end of Truro Station on September 25th, 1961.
*WT Stubbs Collection*

## 83G PENZANCE

**Location**: The shed is north of the line, east of Penzance Station. (OS Map Ref; SW493313)

**Directions**: Turn right outside of the station into East Terrace (A30) and proceed along for about 1 mile. The shed entrance is on the right hand side.

**Closed**: September 10th, 1962.

**Description**: A brick built 5TS dead ended shed.

**Post Closure History**: *Demolished. Floors partially traceable, a concrete roadway passes over the middle of the site, it is otherwise unused. (1988)*

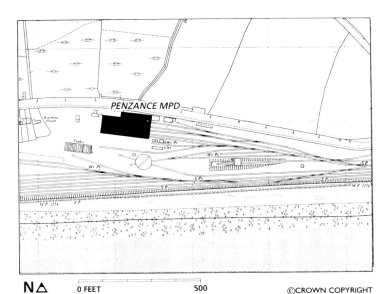

N△    0 FEET    500    ©CROWN COPYRIGHT

**Map Dated**: 1963
**Site Location**: Just east of the roundabout at which point the A30 diverges north towards Redruth.
**Track Status**: Lines are operational.
*The shed was used for diesel purposes until 1976 and was demolished within a year of total closure.*

Warship Class diesel hydraulic locomotives had infiltrated the yard of **PENZANCE MPD** when photographed on September 26th, 1961. Ex-GWR Hall Class 4–6–0 No. 5976 *ASHWICKE HALL* stands by the water column awaiting attention.
*WT Stubbs Collection*

## 83E(s) MOORSWATER

**Location**: The shed is at the end of a Goods Spur, about 0.5 miles north of Coombe Junction Halt. (OS Map Ref; SX236642)

**Directions**: A path leads along the line, from the halt to the shed: Or, alternatively, a road on the south side of the Liskeard to Bodmin Road (A38), about 1 mile west of Liskeard also leads to the shed.

**Closed**: September 1960.

**Description**: A stone built 2TS dead ended shed

*Post Closure History: Demolished. Now site of 'Moorswater Industrial Estate'. The old branch to the China Clay Works is still in use. (1989)*

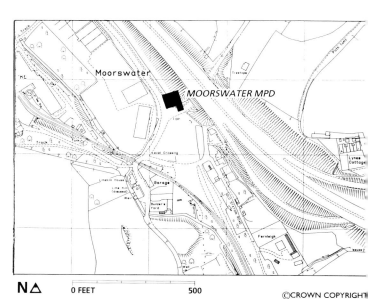

The former Liskeard and Looe Railway shed at **MOORSWATER** on May 26th, 1957.
*WT Stubbs Collection*

**Map Dated**: 1979 (Shed Superimposed)

**Site Location**: On the south west side of Liskeard, adjacent to the A38 bypass.

**Track Status**: Some lines are operational.

## 72D(s) CALLINGTON

**Location**: The shed is north of the line, at the east end of Callington Station. (OS Map Ref; SX361715)

**Directions**: Entrance to the shed is effected from the station platform.

**Closed**: September 1964

**Description**: A corrugated iron 2TS dead ended shed.

*Post Closure History: The shed was demolished shortly after closure and the whole station site is now a Lorry Park. A portakabin style office is sited where the shed was. (1988)*

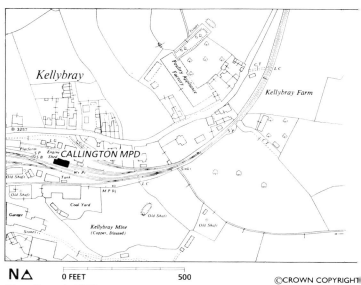

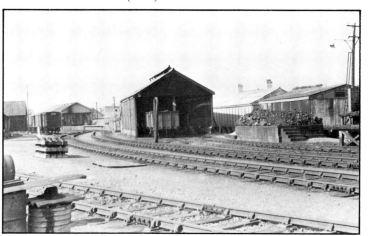

A deserted **CALLINGTON MPD**, photographed on September 25th, 1961.
*WT Stubbs Collection*

**Map Dated**: 1953

**Site Location**: At Kellybray, about one mile north of the town at the junction of the A388 and B3257 roads.

**Track Status**: Callington Station closed in 1966. Site demolished and all track lifted.

## 83E(s) BODMIN

**Location**: The shed is at the south end of Bodmin GW Station, west of the line. (OS Map Ref; SX073662)

**Directions**: Entrance to the shed is effected from the station platform.

**Closed**: April 1962.

**Description**: A stone built 1TS dead ended shed

**Post Closure History**: *Acquired by the GWS (SW Group) for a while, but had to be abandoned and was later demolished. The floor and pits are still intact, complete with rails but severed from the running line. The station and shed site is now operated by the Bodmin & Wenford Railway Preservation Group and there are long term plans to rebuild the shed. (1988)*

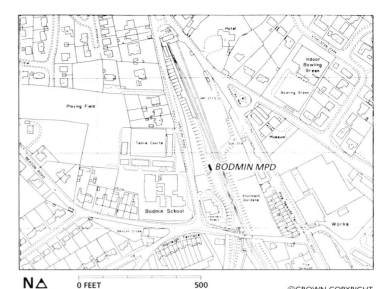

**N△**  0 FEET — 500  ©CROWN COPYRIGHT

**Map Dated**: 1981 (Shed Superimposed)

**Site Location**: In the south of the town, adjacent to the west side of Lostwithiel Road (B3269).

An immaculately tidy **BODMIN MPD**, photographed on July 17th, 1958.

*Alec Swain*

## 83G(s) HELSTON

**Location**: The shed is west of the line, north of Helston Station. (OS Map Ref; SW662281)

**Directions**: Entrance to the shed is effected from the station platform.

**Closed**: December 1963

**Description**: A stone built 1TS dead ended shed.

**Post Closure History**: *The whole station site has been redeveloped. The Goods Shed is now incorporated in an imaginative housing scheme and part of the south end of the station platform is in its garden. The shed site itself is now buried under the northern end of Station Road. (1988)*

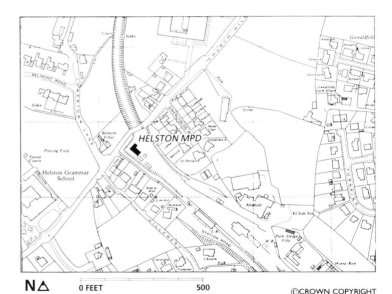

**N△**  0 FEET — 500  ©CROWN COPYRIGHT

**Map Dated**: 1968

**Site Location**: In the north east of the town. Station Road leads north-wards off Godolphin Road (A394).

**Track Status**: Helston Station closed in 1962. Lines lifted.

**HELSTON MPD** on May 26th, 1957. *WT Stubbs Collection*

## 72F WADEBRIDGE

**Location**: The shed is at the north east end of Wadebridge Station. (OS Map Ref; SW992723)

**Directions**: Entrance to the shed is effected from the station platform.

**Closed**: October 1964

**Description**: A brick and timber built 2TS shed with 1 through road.

*Post Closure History*: *Demolished. Now site of a small housing estate. The station and Goods Shed still remain, renovated as the 'John Betjeman Centre' (1988)*

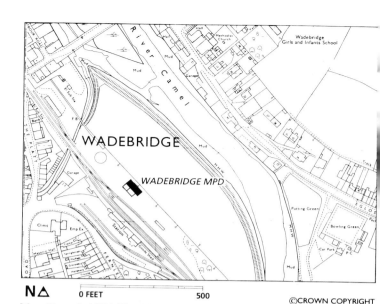

N△  0 FEET  500  ©CROWN COPYRIGHT

**Map Dated:** 1974 (Shed Superimposed)

**Site Location:** In the south of the town, west of the River Camel. The Platt runs south from Molesworth Street (A39).

**Track Status:** Wadebridge Station closed in 1967. Lines lifted.
*The shed was demolished in February 1969.*

**WADEBRIDGE MPD** was home for the three famed Beattie Class 0298 2–4–0WT locomotives. No. 30585 was to the fore when photographed on May 26th, 1957.
*WT Stubbs Collection*

## 72A(s) BUDE

**Location**: The shed is west of the line, at the south end of Bude Station. (OS Map Ref; SS210058)

**Directions**: Entrance to the shed is effected from the station platform.

**Closed**: September 1964

**Description**: A brick built 1TS through road shed.

*Post Closure History*: *The whole site has been cleared and a small housing estate occupies the station area. The bridge carrying the wharf branch over a small river is still in situ and the shed site itself, now part of Kingshill Industrial Estate, is levelled but unused. (1988)*

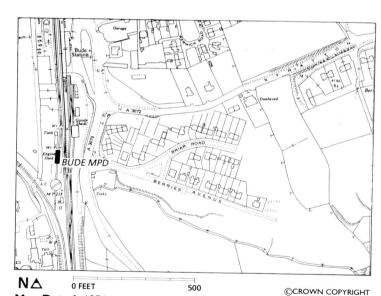

N△  0 FEET  500  ©CROWN COPYRIGHT

**Map Dated:** 1956

**Site Location:** In the south of the town adjacent to the junction of Kings Hill and Stratton Road (A3072).

**Track Status:** Bude Station closed in 1966. Site demolished and all track lifted.

*The shed had been demolished by August 1968*

A solid looking **BUDE MPD** building, photographed on September 26th, 1961.
*WT Stubbs Collection*

## 72A(s) LAUNCESTON (LSWR)

**Location**: The shed is south of the line, at the east end of Launceston (SR) Station. (OS Map Ref; SX332850)
**Directions**: Entrance to the shed is effected from the station platform.
**Out of Use**: 1966
**Description**: A corrugated iron ITS through road shed.
**Post Closure History**: *Demolished. Now part of 'Newport Industrial Estate'. The station site is now a car park for the Launceston Steam Railway and the shed site itself is buried under a roadway. (1988)*

Ex-GWR 0–6–0PT No. 4686 chugs past the remains of **LAUNCESTON (LSWR) MPD** on September 25th, 1961.                    *WT Stubbs Collection*

## 83D(s) LAUNCESTON (GWR)

**Location**: The shed is south of the line, east of Launceston (GWR) Station. (OS Map Ref; SX332850)
**Directions**: Entrance to the shed is effected from the station platform.
**Closed**: December 31st, 1962.
**Description**: A stone built ITS dead ended shed.
**Post Closure History**: *Demolished. Now part of 'Newport Industrial Estate'. The shed site is now buried under industrial units. (1988)*

**LAUNCESTON (GWR) MPD** photographed from the ex-SR goods yard on September 25th, 1961.                    *WT Stubbs Collection*

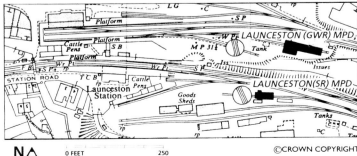

## 83E ST.BLAZEY

**Location**: The shed is west of the goods line between Par Harbour and its junction with the Par to Luxylan line, near St.Blazey Station. (OS Map Ref; SX073538)
**Directions**: Turn right outside of Par Station along a cinder path, turn right at the end and proceed under a bridge and over a level crossing. Bear right and the shed entrance is a gate on the right hand side.
**Closed**: April 1962 (Steam)
**Description**: A brick built semi-roundhouse shed with 9 stalls.
**Post Closure History**: *Used as a Diesel Depot (Code BZ) until April 25th, 1987 when locomotives transferred to the Workshop buildings. The buildings have a Preservation Order on them and are being converted to industrial units. The track will remain in situ and the integrity of the structure will not be altered. The turntable is still in situ. (1988)*

Ex-GWR 0–6–0PT No. 7446 stands on one of the stall roads at **ST.BLAZEY MPD** on May 26th, 1957.                    *WT Stubbs Collection*

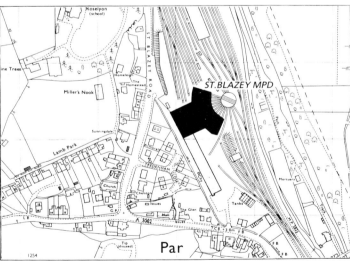

**Map Dated**: 1970
**Site Location**: In the south west of the town, adjacent to the east side of St.Blazey Road (A3082).
**Track Status**: Par Station and lines are operational.
*The building just north of the steam shed, the old workshop, was refurbished and became St.Blazey Diesel Depot in April 1987.*

◀Map Dated: 1953
**Site Location**: In the north of the town, adjacent to east side of St.Thomas Road (A388).
**Track Status**: Launceston (GW) Station closed in 1952, Launceston (SR) in 1966. All lines lifted.

# SOMERSET

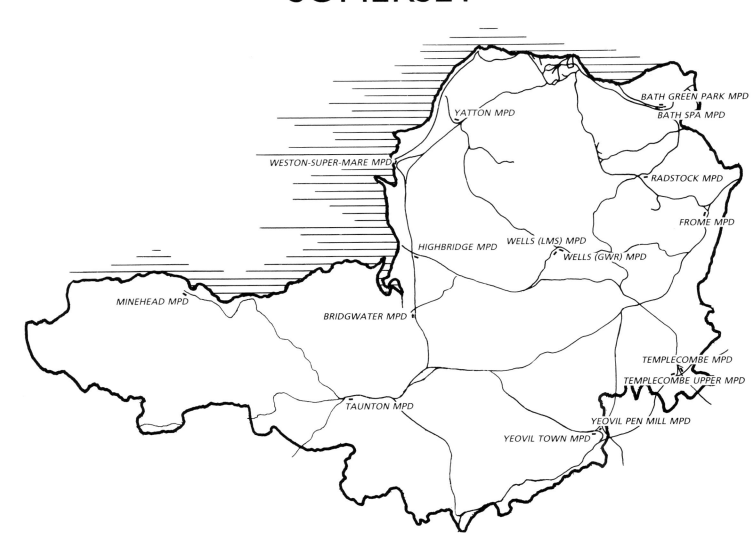

## 83B(s) MINEHEAD

**Location**: The shed is on the south side of Minehead Station. (OS Map Ref; SS975463)

**Directions**: The entrance to the shed is in the Station Yard.

**Closed**: November 3rd, 1956

**Description**: A wooden built 1TS dead ended shed.

*Post Closure History*: *Demolished. Now a Car Park. (1989)*

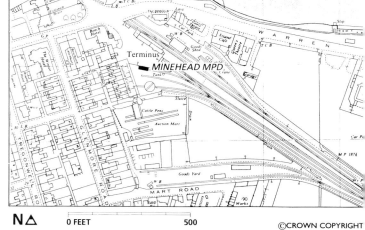

N△   0 FEET          500          ©CROWN COPYRIGHT

**Map Dated:** 1964

**Site Location:** In the town centre, adjacent to the south side of Warren Road.

◄ The small wooden shed at **MINEHEAD**, photographed on July 18th, 1958.

*Alec Swain*

## 71H TEMPLECOMBE

**Location**: The shed is east of the Wincanton to Henstridge line, north of the point where it passes under the main Waterloo to Exeter line. (OS Map Ref; ST710228)

**Directions**: Turn left outside of Templecombe Upper (SR) Station along the approach road, turn left under the bridge, first right before another bridge and the shed entrance is a broad pathway on the left hand side.

**Closed**: March 7th, 1966.

**Description**: Originally a wooden 2TS dead ended shed, later rebuilt by BR in brick.

*Post Closure History: Still Standing. In industrial use by Plessey Marine. (1988)*

**Map Dated:** 1952

**Site Location:** The station is in the middle of the village, just west of the A357.

**Track Status:** Templecombe Upper Station and line are operational. Templecombe Lower closed in 1966. Lines lifted.

*Templecombe MPD was abandoned after closure until the mid-70s. By September 1978 it had been integrated into the Plessey Marine Research Unit.*

TEMPLECOMBE UPPER MPD

## 72C(s) TEMPLECOMBE UPPER

**Location**; The shed is north of the line, west of Templecombe Upper (SR) Station. (OS Map Ref; ST701222)

**Directions**: Entrance to the shed is effected from the station platform.

**Out of Use**: 1951

**Description**: A wooden built 1TS dead ended shed.

*Post Closure History: Demolished. Site Unused. (1988)*

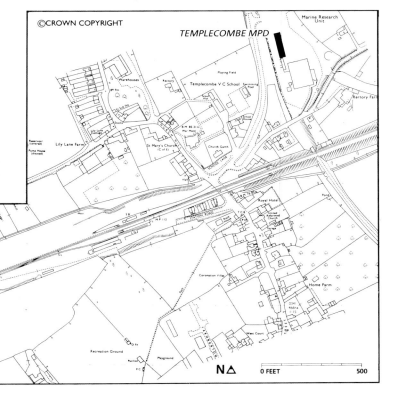

TEMPLECOMBE MPD

©CROWN COPYRIGHT

N△    0 FEET    500

## 82D(s) FROME

**Location**: The shed is west of the line, south of Frome Station. (OS Map Ref; ST784476)

**Directions**: Access to the shed is effected from the station, through the small goods yard.

**Closed**: September 1963

**Description**: A wooden built 1TS dead ended shed

*Post Closure History: Demolished*

**FROME MPD** plays host to Ex-GWR 4500 Class 2–6–2T No. 4572 on July 4th, 1954.
*WT Stubbs Collection*

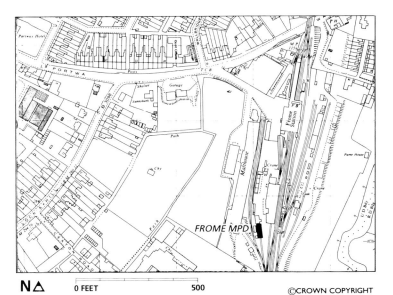

FROME MPD

N△    0 FEET    500    ©CROWN COPYRIGHT

**Map Dated:** 1968 (Shed Superimposed)

**Site Location:** In the south east of the town, adjacent to Wallbridge (A362).

**Track Status:** Frome Station and line are operational.

## 71J HIGHBRIDGE

**Location**: The shed is part of Highbridge Works situated on the south side of the line, east of Highbridge (S&D) Station. (OS Map Ref; ST327467)

**Directions**: Entrance to the works is effected from the station platform.

**Closed**: May 11th, 1959.

**Description**: A brick built 2TS through road shed situated alongside the main works buildings.

**Post Closure History**: *The whole works site has been demolished and flattened. Site Unused. (1972)*

Located within Highbridge Works the right hand portion of this building formed **HIGHBRIDGE MPD**. Photographed, typically without a locomotive in sight, during the late 1950s.                                    *WT Stubbs Collection*

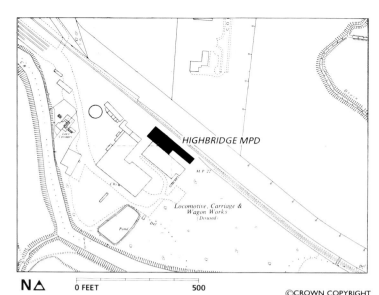

N△    0 FEET    500                    ©CROWN COPYRIGHT

**Map Dated:** 1969 (Shed Superimposed)

**Site Location:** East of the town, adjacent to the B3139

**Track Status:** Highbridge (S&D) Station closed in 1966. S&D line lifted. Highbridge (GW) Station and line are operational.

*Although closed the shed was used until March 1966. The site was used by contractors during construction of the M5 (which passes the east end of the site) in the early 1970s.*

## 71G RADSTOCK NORTH

**Location**: The shed is south of the line, east of Radstock North Station. (OS Map Ref; ST691549)

**Directions**: Turn sharp right outside of the station along a road running parallel to the line, turn right into a rough road crossing the railway and a path leads to the shed from the right hand side.

**Closed**: March 7th, 1966.

**Description**: A stone built 2TS dead ended shed.

**Post Closure History**: *Used by the Somerset & Dorset Trust for a while, but since vacated and the site is now occupied by houses. (1988)*

**RADSTOCK NORTH MPD**, photographed on September 1st, 1961, was the home depot of some of the Sentinel 0–4–0Ts, designed for and employed on lines with tight clearances.                          *WT Stubbs Collection*

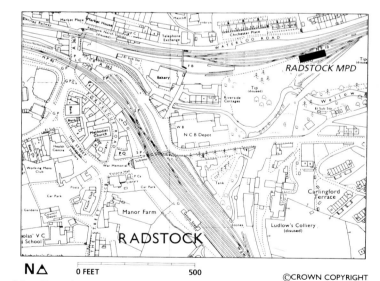

N△    0 FEET    500                    ©CROWN COPYRIGHT

**Map Dated:** 1956

**Site Location:** In the north of the town, east of the junction of the A362 and A367 roads and adjacent to the south side of Waterloo Road.

**Track Status:** Radstock North Station closed in 1966. Lines lifted.

*The shed was demolished in 1980*

## 82A(s) WESTON SUPER MARE

**Location**: The shed is on the south side of Weston super Mare (Locking Road) Station. (OS Map Ref; ST323612)

**Directions**: Turn left outside of the station and left again into the Goods Yard. This leads to the shed.

**Closed**: August 1960

**Description**: A stone built ITS through road shed.

*Post Closure History: Demolished. Site used as Car Park.*

Battle of Britain Class 4–6–2 No. 34090 66 *SQUADRON* finds **WESTON SUPER MARE MPD** a bit of a tight squeeze, whilst taking a breather from an ex-Brighton excursion on November 13th, 1955. *Sid Nash*

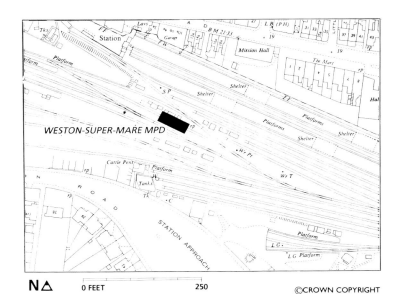

WESTON-SUPER-MARE MPD

N△    0 FEET    250    ©CROWN COPYRIGHT

**Map Dated:** 1953

**Site Location:** In the east of the town, adjacent to the south side of Locking Road (A370).

**Track Status:** Weston Super Mare (Locking Road) Station closed in 1964. Lines lifted. Weston Super Mare Station is operational.

## 82A(s) YATTON

**Location**: The shed is north of the Clevedon Branch, west of Yatton Station. (OS Map Ref; ST423661)

**Directions**: Entrance to the shed is effected from the station platform.

**Closed**: August 1960

**Description**: A stone built ITS dead ended shed.

*Post Closure History: Demolished. Site Unused. (1988)*

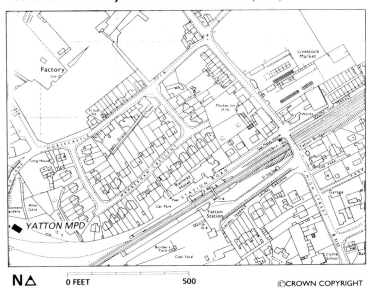

YATTON MPD

N△    0 FEET    500    ©CROWN COPYRIGHT

**Map Dated:** 1977 (Shed Superimposed)

**Site Location:** In the west of the town, Yatton Station is adjacent to High Street (B3133).

**Track Status:** Yatton Station and the main line are operational.

## 83B TAUNTON

**Location**: The shed is south of the line, at the west end of Taunton Station. (OS Map Ref; ST226254)

**Directions**: A gate on the westbound platform, at the west end of the station is the shed entrance.

**Closed**: October 1964.

**Description**: A brick built roundhouse.

*Post Closure History: Was still standing until at least 1972. It has since been demolished, although some of the walls remain and the floors are still traceable. (1989)*

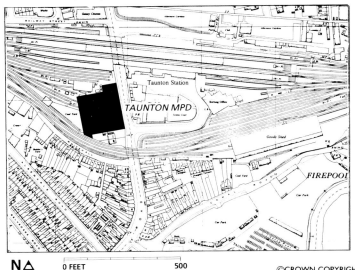

Taunton Station

TAUNTON MPD

FIREPOOL

N△    0 FEET    500    ©CROWN COPYRIGHT

**Map Dated:** 1961

**Site Location:** In the centre of the town, adjacent to Station Road and north of the River Tone.

## 71G BATH GREEN PARK

**Location**: The shed is on the north side of the line, west of Bath Green Park Station. (OS Map Ref; ST742648)

**Directions**: Turn right outside Green Park Station, along Midland Bridge Road, turn right into Lower Bristol Road and right again into Bridge Road. A cinder path leads to the shed from the right hand side of this road just past the railway bridge.

**Closed**: March 7th, 1966.

**Description**: A wooden built 4TS dead ended shed (ex-SDJR) and a stone built 2TS dead ended shed (ex-MR).

*Post Closure History*: *Demolished. The site is now buried under commercial development.*

N△  0 FEET      500                    ©CROWN COPYRIGHT

**Map Dated:** 1968 (Shed Superimposed)

**Site Location:** North of town centre, on the north side of Lower Bristol Road (A36) and adjacent to the west bank of the River Avon.

**Track Status:** Bath Green Park Station closed in 1966. Lines are lifted

## 82A(s) BATH SPA

**Location**: The shed is north of the line, west of Bath Spa (GW) Station. (OS Map Ref; ST744644)

**Directions**: Turn left outside of the station along Dorchester Street and continue into Broad Quay. Turn left over the bridge, right at the end along Lower Bristol Road and the entrance to the Goods Yard is on the left hand side, just past the junction with Oak Street. The shed is located at the far end of this yard.

**Closed**: February 1961.

**Description**: A brick built 1TS through road shed.

*Post Closure History*: *Demolished.*

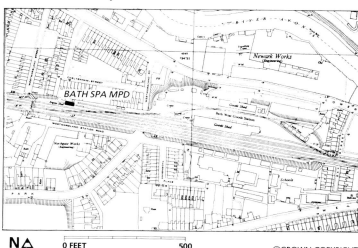

N△  0 FEET      500                    ©CROWN COPYRIGHT

**Map Dated:** 1952

**Site Location:** West of town centre and adjacent to the south side of Lower Bristol Road (A36).

**Track Status:** Bath Spa Station and lines are operational.

## 82E YEOVIL (GWR)

**Location**: The shed is in the fork of the Yeovil Town and Clifton Maybank lines, south of Pen Mill Station. (OS Map Ref; ST563160)

**Directions**: The shed entrance is a gateway on the main road, opposite the end of the approach road to Pen Mill Station.

**Closed**; January 5th, 1959

**Description**: A wooden built 2TS dead ended shed

*Post Closure History*: *Demolished. Site Unused.*

Ex-GWR 0–6–0PT No. 9764 simmers in the yard outside of **YEOVIL (GWR) MPD** on May 19th, 1952.
*John Edgington*

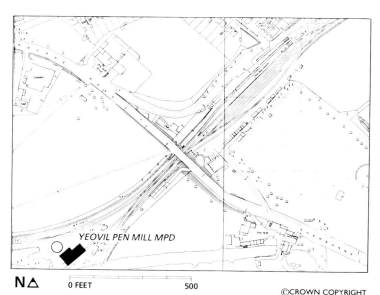

N△  0 FEET      500                    ©CROWN COPYRIGHT

**Map Dated:** 1965 (Shed Superimposed)

**Site Location:** In the north east of the town, adjacent to Sherborne Road (A30).

**Track Status:** Yeovil Pen Mill Station and Westbury to Weymouth line are operational.

*The former line north of the shed which connected Pen Mill and Town Stations is now a walkway.*

## 82A(s) WELLS (GWR)

**Location**: The shed is south of the line, east of Wells (Priory Road) Station. (OS Map Ref; ST546452)
**Directions**: The Wells to Glastonbury Road (A39) crosses the line on the level at the east end of Priory Road Station. Entrance to the shed is effected by means of a path from the east side of this level crossing.
**Closed**: September 9th, 1963.
**Description**: A brick built 2TS through road shed.
*Post Closure History: Demolished. Site Unused. (1972)*

## 71J(s) WELLS (LMS)

**Location**: The shed is south of the Glastonbury line, west of Wells (Priory Road) Station. (OS Map Ref; ST543453)
**Directions**: Entrance to the shed is effected from the station yard.
**Closed**: October 27th, 1951.
**Description**: A stone built 2TS shed with 1 through road.
*Post Closure History: Demolished. Site is part of Industrial Premises.*

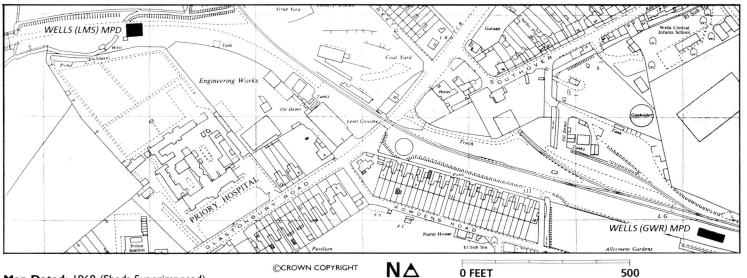

©CROWN COPYRIGHT

**N△**   0 FEET   500

**Map Dated:** 1968 (Sheds Superimposed)
**Site Location:** On the south side of the town, Priory Road (A39) bisects the two sites
**Track Status:** Wells (Priory Road) Station closed in 1951. Lines lifted.

## 72C YEOVIL TOWN

**Location**: The shed is on the south side of Yeovil Town Station. (OS Map Ref; ST563158)
**Directions**: Entrance to the shed is effected from the station platform.
**Closed**: June 1965.
**Description**: A brick built 3TS dead ended shed.
*Post Closure History: Demolished. The whole site is now a Car Park.*

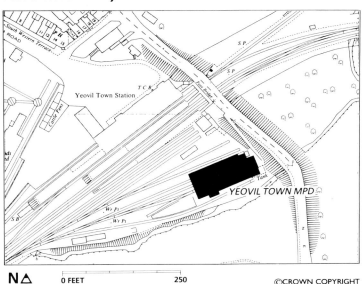

**N△**   0 FEET   250   ©CROWN COPYRIGHT

**Map Dated:** 1963
**Site Location:** In the south east of the town, adjacent to the west side of Newton Road.
**Track Status:** Yeovil Town Station closed in 1966. Lines lifted.

## 83B(s) BRIDGWATER

**Location**: The shed is on the west side of the line, south of Bridgwater GW Station. (OS Map Ref; ST308363)
**Directions**:Turn left out of the station along the approach road, continue into St.John Street and turn first left. Turn right into Colley Lane and then left into Parrett Way. The entrance to the workshops is on the left hand side, and the shed is at the far end of this site.
**Closed**: July 1960
**Description**: An unusual brick built 1TS through road shed, consisting of the last bay of a Carriage Workshop, latterly detached from the remainder of the building.
*Post Closure History: Still Standing. (1987)*

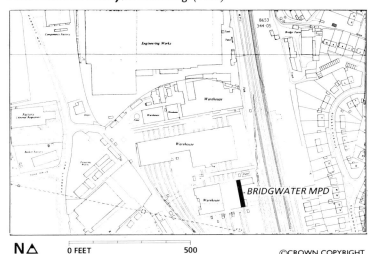

**N△**   0 FEET   500   ©CROWN COPYRIGHT

**Map Dated:** 1969
**Site Location:** In the south east of the town.
**Track Status:** Bridgwater Station and line are operational.

# DORSET

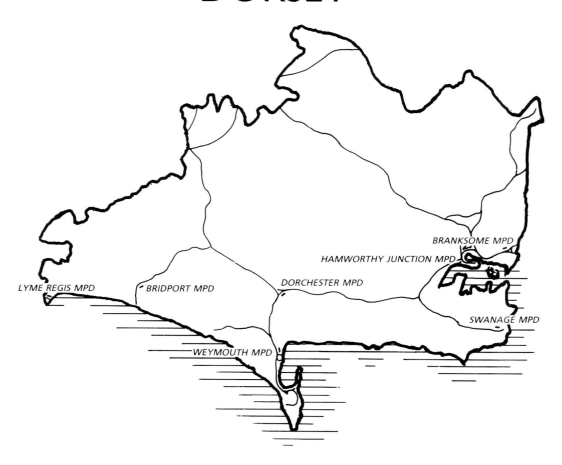

## 71G(s) BRANKSOME

**Location**; The shed is in the fork of the Bournemouth West to Bournemouth Central and the Bournemouth West to Branksome lines.(OS Map Ref; SZ063919)

**Directions**; Turn left outside of Branksome Station into Poole Road and left into Bourne Valley Road. A drive leads through the Goods Yard to the shed from a gate on the right hand side, between the railway overbridges.

**Closed**: August 2nd, 1965.

**Description**: A wooden framed asbestos built 2TS shed with 1 through road.

*Post Closure History: Demolished 1965. Site now in use as a Coal Yard. (1988)*

**Map Dated**: 1944

**Site Location**: West of Bournemouth on the north side of Poole Road (A35).

**Track Status**: Branksome Station and line are operational

©CROWN COPYRIGHT

◀A Standard Class 5 4–6–0 takes on water in the small shed yard of **BRANKSOME MPD** on September 29th, 1961.

*WT Stubbs Collection*

## 71B(s) SWANAGE

**Location**: The shed is north of the line, at the west end of Swanage Station. (OS Map Ref; SZ026789)

**Directions**: Entrance to the shed is effected from the station platform.

**Out of Use**: September 1966

**Description**: A stone built 1TS through road shed.

*Post Closure History: Still Standing.*

The odd layout of **SWANAGE MPD** is clearly illustrated in this photograph, taken on September 29th, 1961. *WT Stubbs Collection*

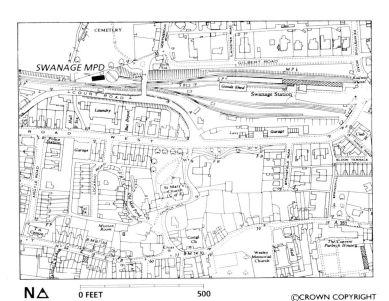

N△    0 FEET    500    ©CROWN COPYRIGHT

**Map Dated**: 1955

**Site Location**: In the north of the town, adjacent to the north side of Court Road.

**Track Status**: Swanage Station closed in 1972, now occupied by Swanage Railway Society.

*The shed has been restored to its former state. A replacement turntable was obtained from Neasden (LT) Shed and the depot re-opened in May 1985.*

## 82F WEYMOUTH

**Location**: The shed is east of the line, north of Weymouth Station. (OS Map Ref; SY675807)

**Directions**: Turn left outside of the station along Queens Street, left into Ranelagh Street and proceed along the pathway running parallel to the line. A cinder path leads to the shed from the left hand side.

**Closed**: July 9th, 1967.

**Description**: A brick built 4TS shed with 3 through roads.

*Post Closure History: Demolished 1971. Now site of Housing Estate. (1988)*

A busy scene at **WEYMOUTH MPD** with ex-GWR Grange Class 4-6-0 No. 6831 *BEARLEY GRANGE* straddling the ash pit on September 28th, 1961. *WT Stubbs Collection*

N△    0 FEET    500    ©CROWN COPYRIGHT

**Map Dated**: 1957

**Site Location**: In the north of the town, west of Dorchester Road (A354)

**Track Status**: Weymouth Station and lines are operational.

*The depot closed completely in October 1970 and the housing estate was completed in 1974.*

## 82F(s) BRIDPORT

**Location**: The shed is east of the line, east of Bridport Station. (OS Map Ref; SY473932)

**Directions**: Entrance to the shed is effected from the station platform.

**Closed**: June 15th, 1959.

**Description**: A stone built 1TS dead ended shed.

***Post Closure History***: *Demolished. Site now in use as a Garden Centre. (1988)*

The stone built **BRIDPORT MPD** on September 28th, 1961, still looking fully utilised although officially closed nearly two years previously.

*WT Stubbs Collection*

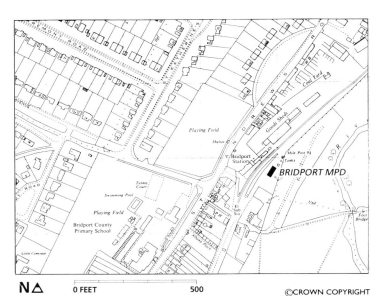

N△   0 FEET   500   ©CROWN COPYRIGHT

**Map Dated:** 1968

**Site Location:** North east of the village, adjacent to St.Andrew's Road (A3066).

**Track Status:** Bridport Station closed in 1975 and the trackbed is now a roadway.

## 72A(s) LYME REGIS

**Location**: The shed is east of the line, at the north end of Lyme Regis Station. (OS Map Ref; SY335925)

**Directions**: Entrance to the shed is effected from the station platform.

**Closed**: November 27th, 1965

**Description**; A wooden and asbestos sheeting built 1TS dead ended shed.

***Post Closure History***; *Demolished. Site now occupied by bungalows. (1989)*

The ramshackle asbestos **LYME REGIS MPD** building on September 28th, 1961.

*WT Stubbs Collection*

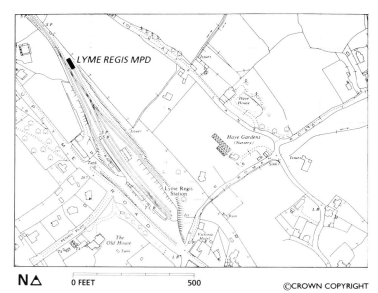

N△   0 FEET   500   ©CROWN COPYRIGHT

**Map Dated:** 1959

**Site Location:** In the north west of the town on the north side of Uplyme Road.

**Track Status:** Lyme Regis Station closed in 1965. Lines lifted.

## 71B(s) HAMWORTHY JUNCTION

**Location**: The shed is in the fork of the Dorchester and Poole lines, west of Hamworthy Junction Station. (OS Map Ref; SY986915)
**Directions**: Entrance to the shed is effected from the station platform.
**Closed**: May 1954.
**Description**: A brick built 1TS through road shed.
*Post Closure History: Used as a store, but later demolished.*

©CROWN COPYRIGHT

**Map Dated:** 1955▶
**Site Location:** North west of Poole. Junction Road leads from the west side of Blandford Road (A350).
**Track Status:** Hamworthy (Junction) Station and main line are operational.

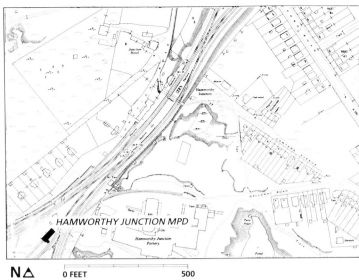

N△    0 FEET    500

## 71C DORCHESTER

**Location**: The shed is east of Dorchester (SR) Station, on the south side of the line. (OS Map Ref; SY693905)
**Directions**: Entrance to the shed is effected from the station platform.
**Closed**: June 17th, 1957
**Description**: A small shed complex of two 2TS dead ended sheds, one built of brick, the other wooden.
*Post Closure History: Demolished. Now site of Housing Estate. (1985)*

©CROWN COPYRIGHT

**Map Dated:** 1956▶
**Site Location:** In the south east of the town, adjacent to Weymouth Avenue (A354).
**Track Status:** Dorchester Station and line are operational.
*The buildings were demolished in 1957.*

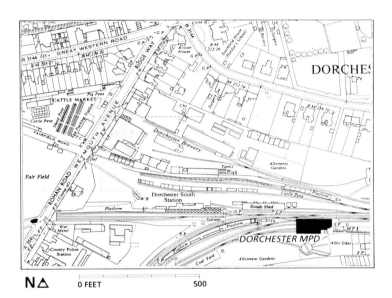

N△    0 FEET    500

# ENGINE SHED SOCIETY

For those interested in depots, the Engine Shed Society was formed in 1986 to bring together railway enthusiasts of a like mind. Through its quarterly magazine, LINK, members are kept up to date on shed developments and in-depth articles on shed related subjects feature in each issue. If sheds are your special interest then this society, with its nominal membership fee, may well be of interest. Please contact the author, through the publishers address if further details are required.

**BOGNOR MPD** (WT Stubbs Collection)

# DEVON

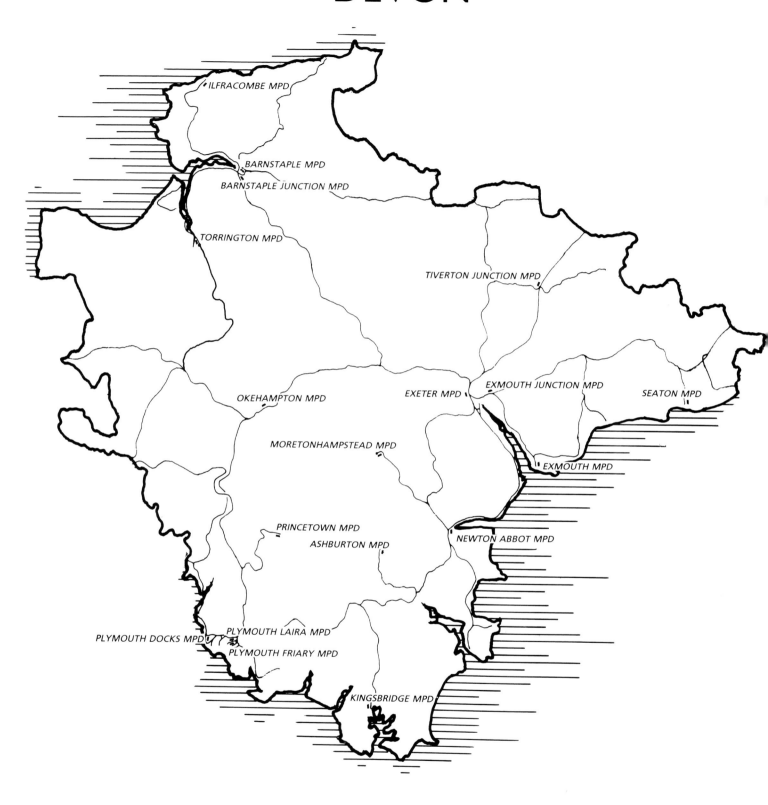

ILFRACOMBE MPD

BARNSTAPLE MPD

BARNSTAPLE JUNCTION MPD

TORRINGTON MPD

TIVERTON JUNCTION MPD

OKEHAMPTON MPD

EXETER MPD

EXMOUTH JUNCTION MPD

SEATON MPD

MORETONHAMPSTEAD MPD

EXMOUTH MPD

PRINCETOWN MPD

ASHBURTON MPD

NEWTON ABBOT MPD

PLYMOUTH DOCKS MPD

PLYMOUTH LAIRA MPD

PLYMOUTH FRIARY MPD

KINGSBRIDGE MPD

## 72A(s) SEATON

**Location**: The shed is on the east side of Seaton Station (OS Map Ref; SY251900)

**Directions**: Entrance to the shed is effected from the station platform.

**Closed**: November 1963.

**Description**: A concrete block built 1TS dead ended shed.

***Post Closure History***: *The whole site has been demolished and is now occupied by a Car Park. (1988)*

The concrete built **SEATON MPD** hosts a coal wagon on September 28th, 1961. *WT Stubbs Collection*

N△        0 FEET        500        ©CROWN COPYRIGHT

**Map Dated:** 1959

**Site Location:** In the east of the town, on the west bank of the River Axe and adjacent to Axmouth Road (B3172)

**Track Status:** Seaton Station closed in 1966 and is now part of the Seaton and Colyford Electric Railway a 2ft 9in gauge tramway which operates along the trackbed.

## 72A(s) EXMOUTH

**Location**: The shed is on the east side of Exmouth Station. (OS Map Ref; SY000811)

**Directions**: Entrance to the shed is effected from the eastern side of the station.

**Closed**: November 1963.

**Description**: A dead ended 1TS shed constructed with concrete blocks.

***Post Closure History***: *Demolished. Now site of roadway (1988)*

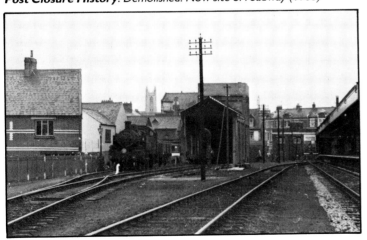

The compact shed layout of **EXMOUTH MPD** photographed on September 25th, 1961. *WT Stubbs Collection*

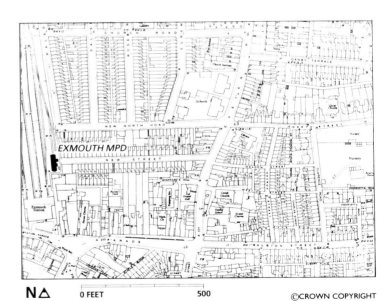

N△        0 FEET        500        ©CROWN COPYRIGHT

**Map Dated:** 1952

**Site Location:** On the east bank of the River Exe in the west of the town, at the end of New Street.

**Track Status:** Exmouth Station and line are operational.

## 83A(s) ASHBURTON

**Location**: The shed is east of the line on the south side of Ashburton Station. (OS Map Ref; SX756697)

**Directions**: Entrance to the shed is effected from the station platform.

**Closed**: November 1958.

**Description**: A stone built 1TS dead-ended shed

*Post Closure History: Still standing and in use as a store (1975)*

Although the branch line was still operational on September 24th, 1961, **ASHBURTON MPD** had been sold for private use as witness the new extension at the front end of the shed building.                    *WT Stubbs Collection*

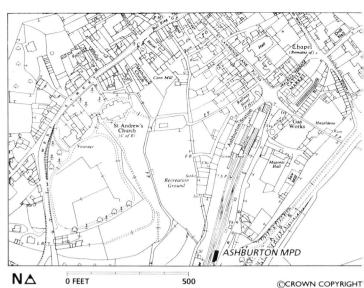

N△        0 FEET        500        ©CROWN COPYRIGHT

**Map Dated:** 1955

**Site Location:** In the south of the town, at the end of St.Lawrence Lane which runs southwards from East Street.

**Track Status:** Ashburton Station was closed in 1958 and the line was totally closed on September 7th, 1962. Lines lifted.

## 83D(s) PLYMOUTH DOCKS

**Location**: The shed is on the west side of the docks branch, about 200 yards south of Millbay Station. (OS Map Ref; SX469540)

**Directions**: Entrance to the shed is effected from the level crossing in Millbay Road, adjacent to the entrance to Millbay Station..

**Out of Use**: c1955

**Description**: A stone built 1TS dead-ended shed.

*Post Closure History: Still Standing in excellent condition. In use as a Maintenance Workshop for the Dock Company. (1988)*

**PLYMOUTH    DOCKS    MPD**    in    private    use    on    October    1st, 1988.                                                              *Paul Smith*

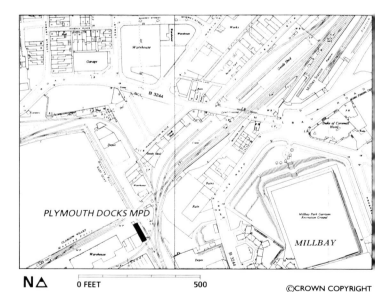

N△        0 FEET        500        ©CROWN COPYRIGHT

**Map Dated:** 1961

**Site Location:** In the south of the city adjacent to the west side of West Hoe Road (B3244).

**Track Status:** Millbay Station closed in 1941. Lines lifted (Some track is still in situ in the dockyard roadways.)

## 72D PLYMOUTH FRIARY

**Location**: The shed is south of the Goods line, east of Friary Station. (OS Map Ref; SX497547)

**Directions**: Turn right outside of the station, right again into Tothill Road, left into Knighton Road and right into Bulmer Road. Continue under the railway bridge, turn left into Desborough Road and the shed entrance is on the left hand side.

**Closed**: May 6th, 1963.

**Description**: A brick built 3TS through road shed.

*Post Closure History: Demolished. The whole site is now a UKF Fertiliser Distribution Depot. (1988)*

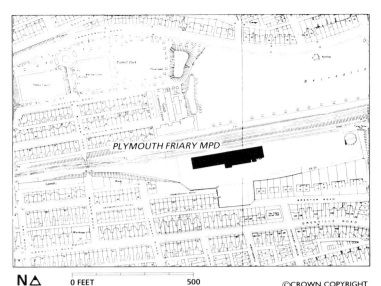

N△  0 FEET  500

**Map Dated**: 1971 (Shed Superimposed)

**Site Location**: In the south east of the city, north of Embankment Road (A374).

**Track Status**: Lucas Terrace Halt closed in 1951. Lines operational

Diesel shunters appear to be the main residents of **PLYMOUTH FRIARY MPD** on September 25th, 1961.

*WT Stubbs Collection*

## 83D PLYMOUTH LAIRA

**Location**: The shed is south of the main line, about 2 miles east of Plymouth Station. (OS Map Ref; SX502557)

**Directions**: Leave Laira Halt, pass under the railway line and this tunnel leads to the shed.

**Closed**: April 1964.

**Description**: A brick built roundhouse with a 4TS through road shed built alongside.

*Post Closure History: Demolished. Now site of sidings for adjacent Diesel Depot (Code LA). (1988)*

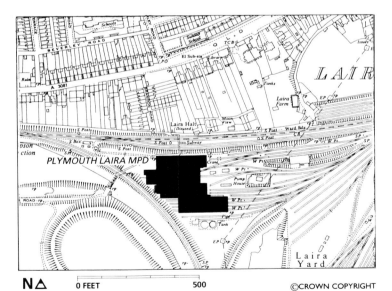

N△  0 FEET  500

**Map Dated**: 1951

**Site Location**: In the south east of the city on the west bank of the River Plym and immediately west of Embankment Road (A374).

**Track Status**: Laira Halt closed in 1930. Lines operational.

A distant view of **PLYMOUTH LAIRA MPD** on September 24th, 1961, showing the approach roads and coaling stage.

*WT Stubbs Collection*

## 72A(s) OKEHAMPTON

**Location**: The shed is north of the line, at the east end of Okehampton Station. (OS Map Ref; SX593945)

**Directions**: Entrance to the shed is effected from the station platform.

**Out of Use**: 1964.

**Description**: A concrete block built 1TS dead ended shed.

**Post Closure History**: *Demolished in 1966. The concrete floor, pits and part of the north wall still remained in 1988. Site Unused.*

The concrete built shed at **OKEHAMPTON** on September 27th, 1961.
*WT Stubbs Collection*

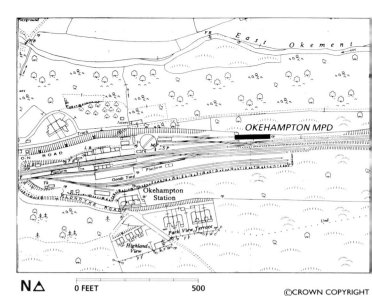

N△    0 FEET         500    ©CROWN COPYRIGHT

**Map Dated**: 1955

**Site Location**: About half a mile south of the town. The road to the station leads off an unclassified road signposted to the Dartmoor National Park and Golf Course.

**Track Status**: The station, although closed in 1972, remains virtually intact with all the buildings adopted for private use. A single line of track passes through the site and is utilised for quarry traffic from Meldon.

## 83C(s) TIVERTON JUNCTION

**Location**: The shed is west of the line, at the south end of Tiverton Junction Station. (OS Map Ref; ST031113)

**Directions**: Entrance to the shed is effected from the station platform.

**Closed**: October 1964.

**Description**: A brick built 1TS dead ended shed.

**Post Closure History**: *Demolished. The site is now part of industrial premises.*

**TIVERTON JUNCTION MPD** on July 18th, 1958.        *Alec Swain*

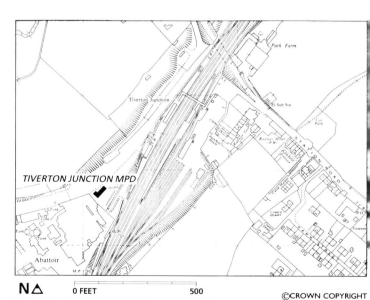

N△    0 FEET         500    ©CROWN COPYRIGHT

**Map Dated**: 1970 (Shed Superimposed)

**Site Location**: Just east of the A38, about four miles north of Cullompton. An elevated section of the M5 passes just west of the site.

**Track Status**: Tiverton Junction Station and main line are operational.

# 72A EXMOUTH JUNCTION

**Location**: The shed is on the north side of the main line, just east of the junction with the Exmouth line. (OS Map Ref; SX940938)

**Directions**: Turn right outside of Polsloe Bridge Halt along the main road, turn left into Beacon Lane and, immediately past a railway bridge, left again along a path running parallel to the line. At the end of this path turn right along another path and left at the end into Prince Charles Road. The shed entrance is on the left hand side a few yards further along.

**Closed**: June 1965

**Description**: A concrete and brick built 15TS dead ended shed.

**Post Closure History**: *Demolished. Now site of 'Leo's Supermarket' (1988)*

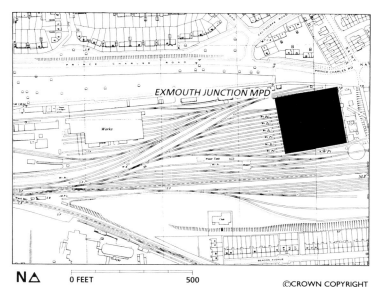

**Map Dated:** 1951

**Site Location:** In the north east of the city, just north of the A3085 and immediately south of Prince Charles Road.

**Track Status:** Polsloe Bridge Halt and lines are operational
*The shed closed completely in March 1967.*

The large shed at **EXMOUTH JUNCTION**, with not a diesel in sight, is clearly illustrated in this photograph taken on September 24th, 1961.
*WT Stubbs Collection*

# 83C EXETER

**Location**: The shed is adjacent to the west side of Exeter St.Davids Station. (OS Map Ref; SX911933)

**Directions**: A boarded crossing leads from the south end of the station platforms to the shed.

**Closed**: October 14th, 1963

**Description**: A brick built 4TS through road shed.

**Post Closure History**: *Partially demolished. In use as a Diesel Depot (Code EX), it was re-roofed in 1987.*

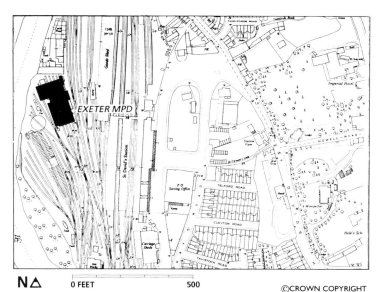

**Map Dated:** 1952

**Site Location:** In the west of the city, adjacent to the east bank of the River Exe and Bonhay Road (B3183)

**Track Status:** Exeter St.David's Station and lines are operational.
*The shed building was roofless from 1963.*

**EXETER MPD** on September 24th, 1961 with a couple of Warship Diesel Hydraulics in the yard.
*WT Stubbs Collection*

## 83A(s) KINGSBRIDGE

**Location**: The shed is south of the line, at the west end of Kingsbridge Station. (OS Map Ref; SX732441)

**Directions**: Entrance to the shed is effected from the station platform.

**Closed**: September 1961.

**Description**: A stone built 1TS dead ended shed.

***Post Closure History***: *Demolished. Now site of Coach Garage. (1988)*

Ex-GWR 4500 Class 2–6–2T No. 5505 stands in the station alongside **KINGSBRIDGE MPD** on August 17th, 1953. *John Edgington*

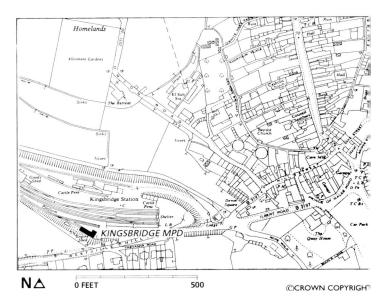

N△   0 FEET   500   ©CROWN COPYRIGHT

**Map Dated:** 1955

**Site Location:** In the west of the town, adjacent to north side of Westville Hill (B3197)

**Track Status:** Kingsbridge Station closed in 1963. Lines lifted.

## 83A NEWTON ABBOT

**Location**: The shed is on the east side of Newton Abbot Station. (OS Map Ref; SX868712)

**Directions**: Turn left outside of the station into Station Road, continue along Torquay Road and turn left after crossing the railway bridge. The shed entrance is on the left hand side of this road.

**Closed**: April 1st, 1962.

**Description**: A stone built 6TS dead ended shed.

***Post Closure History***: *Still Standing, lines lifted and roofless. (1988)*

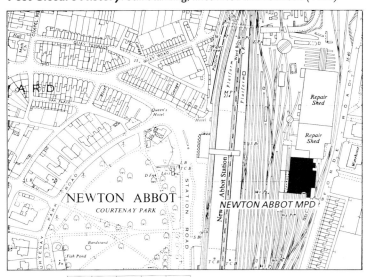

N△   0 FEET   500   ©CROWN COPYRIGHT

**Map Dated:** 1956

**Site Location:** In the east of the town, adjacent to Station Road (A380).

**Track Status:** Newton Abbot Station and line are operational.

## SITE UTILISATIONS (1)

The less accessible sites prove to be of little commercial value and just become forgotten corners and left to their own devices, hence the near-Amazonian rain forest appearance of **ST IVES MPD**. A closer inspection of the site, in 1988 revealed, buried beneath a thick undergrowth, the engine pit full of green water!

*Paul Smith*

## 83A(s) MORETONHAMPSTEAD

**Location**: The shed is west of the line, at the south end of Moretonhampstead Station. (OS Map Ref; SX758856)
**Directions**: Entrance to the shed is effected from the station platform.
**Closed**; November 1947, and subsequently used as a Stabling Point.
**Description**: A stone built 1TS dead ended shed.
*Post Closure History: Still Standing in excellent condition. In use as a Lorry repair depot. (1989)*

**MORETONHAMPSTEAD MPD** appeared to be out of use for locomotive purposes when photographed on September 27th, 1961.

*WT Stubbs Collection*

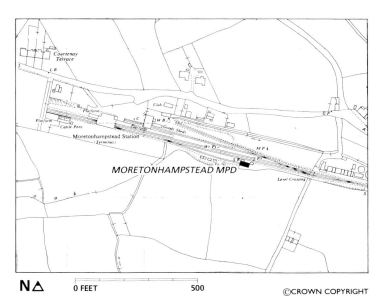

N△    0 FEET    500    ©CROWN COPYRIGHT

**Map Dated:** 1958
**Site Location:** South east of the town, adjacent to the A382.
**Track Status:** Moretonhampstead Station closed in 1959 and the line closed totally on April 6th, 1964. Lines lifted.

## 83D(s) PRINCETOWN

**Location**: The shed is south of the line, adjacent to Princetown Station. (OS Map Ref; SX588735)
**Directions**: Entrance to the shed is effected from the station platform.
**Closed**; March 11th 1956.
**Description**: A stone built 1TS dead ended shed.
*Post Closure History: The whole site has been obliterated and is now grazing land for horses. (1988)*

*"Sheep may safely graze"*. **PRINCETOWN**, devoid of all track with all its buildings in various states of disrepair on June 2nd, 1959. The shed is the building on the right.

*Sid Nash*

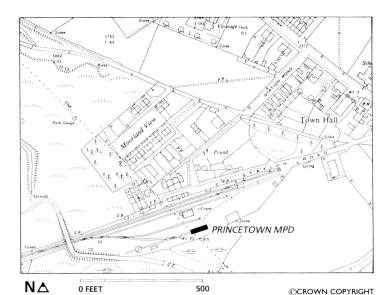

N△    0 FEET    500    ©CROWN COPYRIGHT

**Map Dated:** 1953
**Site Location:** Station Road is just north of the junction of the B3212 and B3357 roads and the station site is in the south part of the town.
**Track Status:** Princetown Station and line closed in March 1956. Lines lifted.

## 72E(s) ILFRACOMBE

**Location**: The shed is east of the line, at the south end of Ilfracombe Station. (OS Map Ref; SS514464)

**Directions**: Entrance to the shed is effected from the station platform.

**Out of Use**: 1964

**Description**: A 1TS through road shed constructed from concrete blocks.

**Post Closure History**: *Demolished shortly after closure.*

The simple concrete built **ILFRACOMBE MPD** photographed on September 27th, 1961.                                    *WT Stubbs Collection*

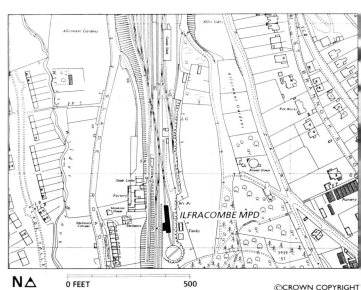

N△          0 FEET                    500          ©CROWN COPYRIGHT

**Map Dated:** 1962

**Site Location:** In the south west of the town, sandwiched between and immediately south of the junction of Brannock's Road (A361) and B3231 roads.

**Track Status:** Ilfracombe Station and line closed in October 1970. Lines lifted.


## 72E(s) TORRINGTON

**Location**: The shed is west of the line, at the north end of Torrington Station. (OS Map Ref; SS479198)

**Directions**: Entrance to the shed is effected from the station platform.

**Closed**: November 2nd, 1959.

**Description**: A wooden built 1TS dead ended shed.

**Post Closure History**: *Demolished. Site Unused. The station is now a pub called the 'Puffing Billy' and the platforms and shed site form part of its back garden! (1988)*

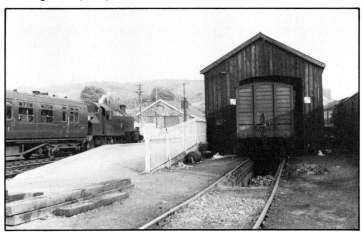

Ex-LMS Ivatt Class 2 2–6–2T No. 41313 stands in the station alongside **TORRINGTON MPD** on June 4th, 1960. The shed had been relegated to use as a siding by this time with the engine pit being slowly filled with rubbish.
*Sid Nash*

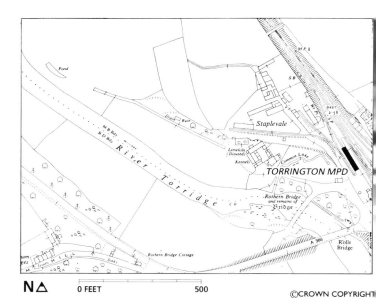

N△          0 FEET                    500          ©CROWN COPYRIGHT

**Map Dated:** 1955

**Site Location:** About one mile west of Great Torrington and adjacent to the point where the A386 crosses the River Torridge.

**Track Status:** Torrington Station closed in 1965. Lines lifted.

## 72E BARNSTAPLE JUNCTION

**Location**: The shed is on the east side of Barnstaple Junction Station. (OS Map Ref; SS556325)

**Directions**: The shed entrance is in the station yard.

**Closed**: September 1964.

**Description**: A wooden built 2TS through road shed, the building was virtually roofless and semi-derelict by the time of closure.

*Post Closure History: Demolished shortly after closure. The shed floor was still traceable and some track was still in situ in the yard as late as 1988.*

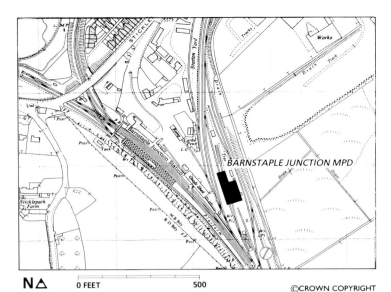

**Map Dated:** 1958

**Site Location:** South of town centre, on the south east side of Sticklepath Terrace (A39).

**Track Status:** Barnstaple Station and line are operational south of the town.

A busy scene at the remnants of **BARNSTAPLE JUNCTION MPD** belies the fact that it was on the eve of closure when photographed on August 30th, 1964.
*Sid Nash*

## 83B(s) BARNSTAPLE

**Location**: The shed is on the south side of the line, east of Barnstaple (GW) Station. (OS Map Ref; SS569326)

**Directions**: Entrance to the shed is effected from the station platform.

**Closed**: January 1951.

**Description**: A wooden built 2TS dead ended shed

*Post Closure History: Demolished. Site Unused. The shed floor was still visible in 1988.*

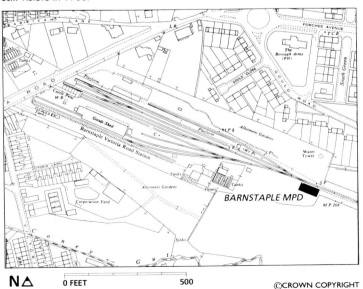

**Map Dated:** 1957 (Shed Superimposed)

**Site Location:** East of town centre adjacent to Victoria Road.

**Track Status:** Barnstaple Victoria Station closed in 1970. Lines lifted

## SITE UTILISATIONS (2)

The larger accessible areas are rapidly taken up for commercial development. In some instances a single concern will occupy the site, but more often they take the form of industrial or business parks. **MOORSWATER MPD** and Works is now the *Moorswater Industrial Estate* and this view, taken in 1988, shows the stone arched viaduct carrying the Plymouth to Penzance line across the site with the roadway crossing the original location of the shed at the bottom of the slope. *Paul Smith*

# PART TWO
# CENTRAL SOUTHERN ENGLAND

## WILTSHIRE    HAMPSHIRE    BERKSHIRE

DIDCOT

SWINDON

BERKSHIRE

READING

WILTSHIRE

BASINGSTOKE

WESTBURY

SALISBURY

HAMPSHIRE

SOUTHAMPTON

PORTSMOUTH

BOURNEMOUTH

RYDE

BRITISH RAILWAYS

**FRATTON MPD** *(Lens of Sutton)*

# BERKSHIRE

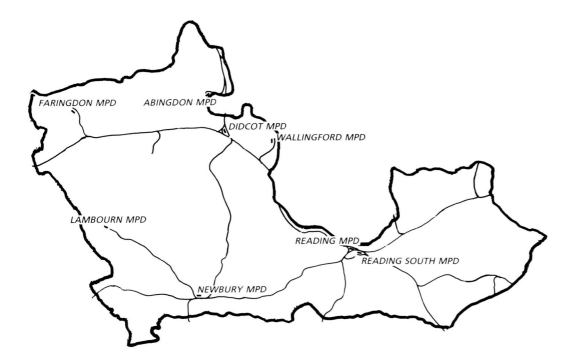

## 81E(s) NEWBURY

**Location**; The shed is north of the line, adjacent to the Lambourn Branch Bay Platform, at the west end of Newbury Station. (OS Map Ref; SU472667)

**Directions**; Entrance to the shed is effected from the station platform.

**Out of Use**; 1960.

**Description**; Consisting of a locomotive stand siding only. There are no shed buildings.

*Post Closure History; Lines lifted.*

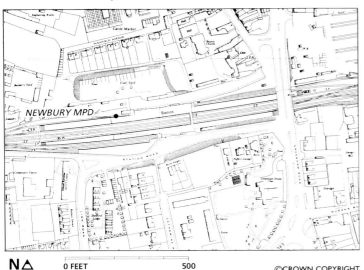

**Map Dated:** 1967

**Site Location:** In the south of the town adjacent to Greenham Road (A3430.

**Track Status:** Newbury Station and lines are operational.

## 81E(s) LAMBOURN

**Location**; The shed is west of the line, at the north end of Lambourn Station. (OS Map Ref; SU328785)

**Directions**; Entrance to the shed is effected from the station platform.

**Closed**; 1937 and subsequently used as a Stabling Point until 1960.

**Description**; Originally a corrugated iron ITS dead ended shed, demolished in March 1940, and by BR days was an engine pit and siding only.

*Post Closure History; The whole site has been demolished*

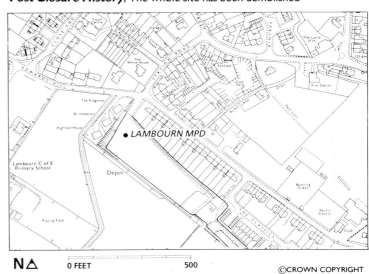

**Map Dated:** 1979

**Site Location:** In the south east of the town. Station Road leads southwards off Newbury Street.

**Track Status:** Lambourn Station and line closed on January 4th, 1960. Lines lifted.

*The entire station site is now occupied by a haulage concern*

## 81D READING

**Location**: The shed is in the fork of the Newbury and Didcot lines, west of Reading General Station. (OS Map Ref; SU707739)

**Directions**: Turn right outside of the station along Tudor Road, turn left into Caversham Road, right into Great Knollys Street and right into Hodsoll Road. A path leads to the shed from the end of this road.

**Closed**: January 4th, 1965 (Steam)

**Description**: A brick built 9TS shed with 4 through roads.

*Post Closure History: Demolished and replaced by a purpose built Diesel Depot (Code RG).*

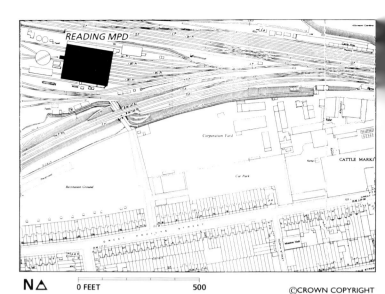

N△    0 FEET    500    ©CROWN COPYRIGHT

**Map Dated:** 1961

**Site Location:** In the centre of the town, just north of Oxford Road (A329)

**Track Status:** Reading General Station and lines are operational.

**READING MPD** with BR Standard Class 9F 2–10–0 No. 92004 in the shed yard on September 19th, 1963.                    *WT Stubbs Collection*

## 70E READING SOUTH

**Location**: The shed is north of the line, east of Reading South Station. (OS Map Ref; SU719738)

**Directions**: Turn left outside of the main entrance to the station and bear left along Blagrave Road. Turn left into Vastern Road, pass under the bridge and the shed entrance is a gate on the right hand side, before the second railway bridge.

**Closed**: January 1965.

**Description**: A brick built 3TS through road shed.

*Post Closure History: Demolished. Now site of Office Blocks. (1989)*

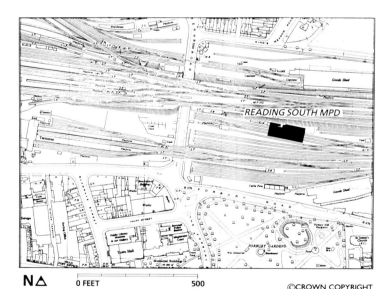

N△    0 FEET    500    ©CROWN COPYRIGHT

**Map Dated:** 1958

**Site Location:** In the centre of the town, just north of the junction of Forbury Road (B479) and Vastern Road (B3345).

**Track Status:** Reading South Station closed in 1965. Lines lifted.

**READING SOUTH MPD** on September 19th, 1963. The signals on the right hand side are on the adjacent ex-GWR Paddington to Bristol main line.
                    *WT Stubbs Collection*

## 81E DIDCOT

**Location**: The shed is on the east side of the Oxford line, north of Didcot Station. (OS Map Ref; SU524908)

**Directions**: Entrance to the shed is effected from the station subway, and via a flight of steps on the north side of the station.

**Closed**: April 5th, 1965

**Description**: A brick and corrugated iron 4TS shed with 3 through roads.

***Post Closure History***: *Preserved as the headquarters of the Great Western Society, Didcot.*

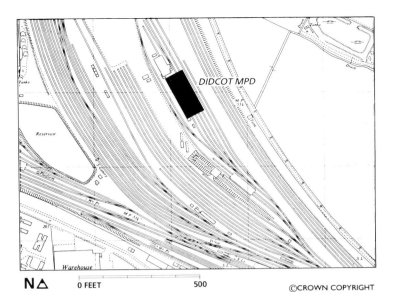

N△   0 FEET   500   ©CROWN COPYRIGHT

**Map Dated:** 1968
**Site Location:** In the north of the town.
**Track Status:** Didcot Station and lines are operational.

**DIDCOT MPD** in BR guise on September 9th, 1962.   *WT Stubbs Collection*

## 81E(s) WALLINGFORD

**Location**: The shed is on the west side of Wallingford Station. (OS Map Ref; SU601895)

**Directions**: Entrance to the shed is effected from the station platform.

**Closed**: February 1956

**Description**: A brick built 1TS dead ended shed.

***Post Closure History***: *Demolished. The whole site is now a housing estate. (1978)*

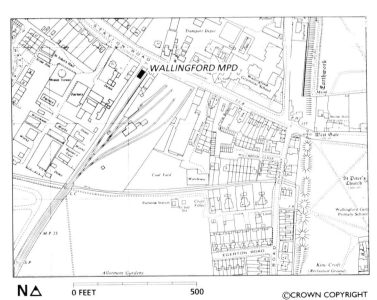

N△   0 FEET   500   ©CROWN COPYRIGHT

**Map Dated:** 1968
**Site Location:** West of the town centre, adjacent to Station Road (A4130).
**Track Status:** Wallingford Station closed for passengers in 1959 and totally on September 13th, 1965. Lines lifted in station area.

**WALLINGFORD MPD** still standing and in use as a store seven years after closure, on September 19th, 1963.   *WT Stubbs Collection*

## 81F(s) ABINGDON

**Location**: The shed is on the south side of the line, east of Abingdon Station. (OS Map Ref; SU499973)

**Directions**: Entrance to the shed is effected from the station platform.

**Closed**: March 20th, 1954

**Description**: A brick built 1TS dead-ended shed.

***Post Closure History***: *Demolished. Site Unused. (1972)*

A slightly indistinct but nonetheless useful pre-war photograph of the small and relatively obscure **ABINGDON MPD**.                                    *W.A.Camwell*

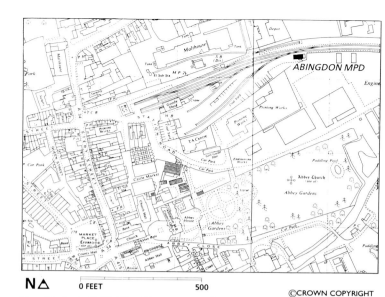

**Map Dated:** 1967 (Shed Superimposed)

**Site Location:** East of town centre, adjacent to the junction of Broad Street and Stert Street (A34).

**Track Status:** The station closed in 1963 but the line was used for freight purposes well into the 1970s.

## 82C(s) FARINGDON

**Location**: The shed is on the west side of the line, adjacent to Faringdon Station. (OS Map Ref; SU288951)

**Directions**: Entrance to the shed is effected from the station platform.

**Closed**: December 1951.

**Description**: A stone built 1TS dead ended shed.

***Post Closure History***: *Still standing until 1975 at least when most of the station buildings and the shed were incorporated in an industrial development. The shed building has since been demolished and new industrial buildings erected. (1988)*

A sense of dereliction pervades the scene on September 27th, 1964 with **FARINGDON MPD** well established as a private garage some 13 years after closure.                                         *WT Stubbs Collection*

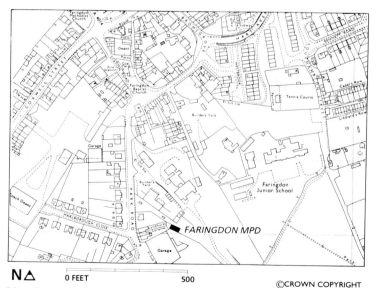

**Map Dated:** 1971

**Site Location:** In the south of the town, adjacent to the east side of Park Road.

**Track Status:** Faringdon Station closed in 1951. Lines lifted.

# WILTSHIRE

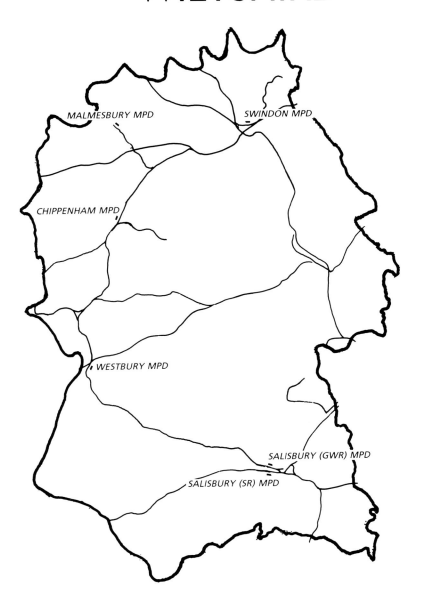

MALMESBURY MPD

SWINDON MPD

CHIPPENHAM MPD

WESTBURY MPD

SALISBURY (GWR) MPD

SALISBURY (SR) MPD

## 82C(s) CHIPPENHAM
**Location**: The shed is on the north side of the line, east of Chippenham Station. (OS Map Ref; ST925741)

**Directions**: Cross the railway by the footbridge adjacent to the station entrance, proceed along Old Road, passing the front of the Old Road Inn, and turn sharp right into Foundry Lane. A cinder path leads to the shed from the end of this lane.

**Closed**: March 2nd, 1964.

**Description**: A stone built 3TS dead ended shed.

*Post Closure History*: Demolished.

**Map Dated**: 1968 (Shed Superimposed) ▶

**Site Location**: North east of the town centre, Foundry Lane runs east-wards from New Road (A420).

**Track Status**: Chippenham Station and line are operational.

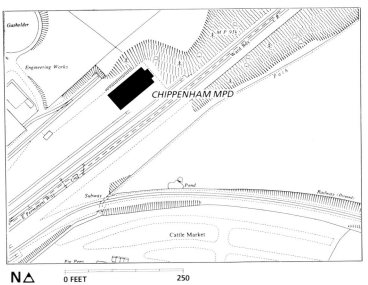

Gasholder

Engineering Works

CHIPPENHAM MPD

Permanent Way

Subway

Pond

Railway (Disused)

Cattle Market

Pig Pens

N △   0 FEET                    250

## 82C SWINDON

**Location**: The shed is north of the Gloucester line, west of Swindon Station. (OS Map Ref; SU143854)

**Directions**: Turn right outside of the station along Station Road, continue along Sheppard Street and London Street. A gate on the right hand side is the official works entrance and a tunnel leads from the works site to the shed.

**Closed**: October 1964.

**Description**: A brick built double roundhouse and 10TS dead ended shed.

*Post Closure History: Stabled diesel locomotives until 1970 and was demolished in the following year. Now site of 'North Star Industrial Estate'. (1989)*

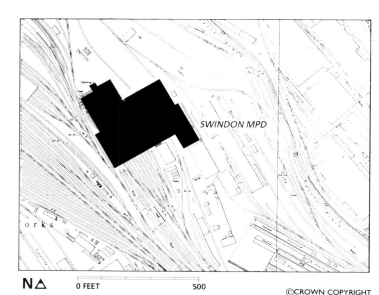

SWINDON MPD

N△   0 FEET        500        ©CROWN COPYRIGHT

**Map Dated**: 1957
**Site Location**: In the east of the town, due south of Ferndale Road.
**Track Status**: Swindon Station and lines are operational.

For a GWR 'top' shed **SWINDON MPD** always seemed to have a sense of semi-dereliction about the buildings during BR days. This view, through the smoke haze, was taken on a chill and dull November 6th, 1960.          *WT Stubbs Collection.*

## 82D WESTBURY

**Location**: The shed is south of the line, west of Westbury Station. (OS Map Ref; ST861518)

**Directions**: A roadway leads to the shed from the west end of the Station Yard.

**Closed**: September 1965.

**Description**: A brick built 4TS through road shed.

*Post Closure History: Demolished. Now site of dump for PW materials. (1988)*

A half empty **WESTBURY MPD** photographed on September 30th, 1961.
*WT Stubbs Collection*

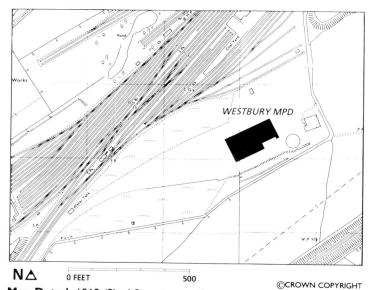

WESTBURY MPD

N△   0 FEET        500        ©CROWN COPYRIGHT

**Map Dated**: 1968 (Shed Superimposed)
**Site Location**: North west of the town.
**Track Status**: Westbury Station and lines are operational.
*The shed had been demolished by 1978*

## 72B SALISBURY

**Location**: The shed is south of the line, west of Salisbury Station. (OS Map Ref; SU129303)

**Directions**: Cross the Station Yard and descend the steps into Churchfields Road. Turn right and continue following the road running parallel to the track. The shed entrance is on the right hand side, at the corner of Cherry Orchard Lane.

**Closed**: July 9th, 1967.

**Description**: A brick built 10TS dead ended shed.

***Post Closure History***: *Demolished in November 1969.*

## 82D(s) SALISBURY (GWR)

**Location**: The shed is north of the line, west of Salisbury (GWR) Station. (OS Map Ref; SU132302)

**Directions**: Cross the Station Yard and descend the steps into Churchfields Road. Turn right and, after a short distance, right again into Ashfield Road. The shed entrance is on the right hand side, just past the bridge.

**Closed**: November 1950.

**Description**: A brick built 3TS dead ended shed.

***Post Closure History***: *Demolished. Now site of 'Ashfield Trading Estate' (1988)*

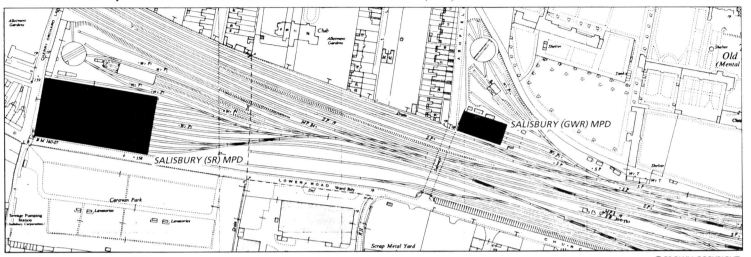

N△    0 FEET    250    ©CROWN COPYRIGHT

**Map Dated:** 1954

**Site Location:** In the west of the town, south of Wilton Road (A30)

**Track Status:** Salisbury Station and line are operational.

## 82C(s) MALMESBURY

**Location**: The shed is east of the line, adjacent to Malmesbury Station. (OS Map Ref; ST935871)

**Directions**: A boarded crossing at the south end of the station leads to the shed.

**Closed**: September 10th, 1951.

**Description**: A stone built 1TS through road shed.

***Post Closure History***: *Still Standing. In industrial use (1970)*

**MALMESBURY MPD**, derelict but intact when photographed on August 21st, 1960, nearly nine years after closure.
*WT Stubbs Collection*

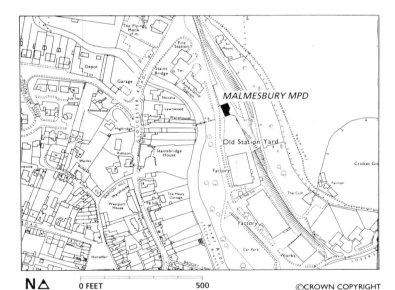

N△    0 FEET    500    ©CROWN COPYRIGHT

**Map Dated:** 1981

**Site Location:** In the north of the town, adjacent to Gloucester Road (B4014) and on the east bank of the River Avon.

**Track Status:** Malmesbury Station closed in 1951. Lines lifted.

# HAMPSHIRE

BASINGSTOKE (SR) MPD
BASINGSTOKE (GWR) MPD
ANDOVER JUNCTION MPD
ANDOVER MPD
WINCHESTER CITY MPD
WINCHESTER CHESIL MPD
EASTLEIGH MPD
SOUTHAMPTON TERMINUS MPD
SOUTHAMPTON NEW DOCKS MPD
SOUTHAMPTON DOCKS MPD
LYMINGTON MPD
GOSPORT MPD
FRATTON MPD
BOURNEMOUTH MPD
NEWPORT (IOW) MPD
RYDE (IOW) MPD

## 71D FRATTON

**Location**: The shed is east of the line, north of Fratton Station. (OS Map Ref; SU657000)

**Directions**: Leave the station by the southern exit, turn left into Goldsmith Avenue, proceed past the car sheds and a cinder path leads to the shed from the left hand side of this road.

**Closed**: November 2nd, 1959

**Description**; A brick built roundhouse.

*Post Closure History: Demolished. Site of NCL depot. (1975)*

**Map Dated:** 1946▶

**Site Location:** In the east of the town, adjacent to north side of Goldsmith Avenue (A2030).

**Track Status:** Fratton Station and lines are operational. *The shed was demolished in 1969.*

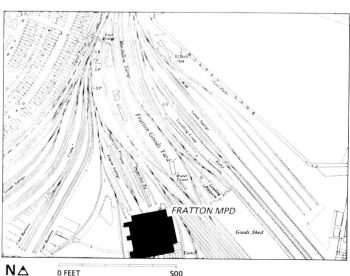

FRATTON MPD

N△     0 FEET     500

## 70D BASINGSTOKE (SR)

**Location**: The shed is on the north side of the line, west of Basingstoke (SR) Station. (OS Map Ref; SU634526)

**Directions**: Go straight ahead outside of the station into Station Hill and turn right into Junction Road, turn right at the end into Chapel Street and fork left under the bridge. The shed entrance is on the left hand side just past the bridge.

**Closed**: March 1963.

**Description**: A brick built 3TS dead-ended shed.

*Post Closure History: Was used as a stabling point after closure, right up to the end of steam in 1967. Completely demolished in 1969.*

## 81D(s) BASINGSTOKE (GWR)

**Location**; The shed is on the north side of the line, at the east end of Basingstoke (GWR) Station. (OS Map Ref; SU639527)

**Directions**; Entrance to the shed is effected from the car park at the rear of the station.

**Closed**; November 1950.

**Description**; A wood and brick built 2TS through road shed.

*Post Closure History; Demolished. Sidings now occupy site.*

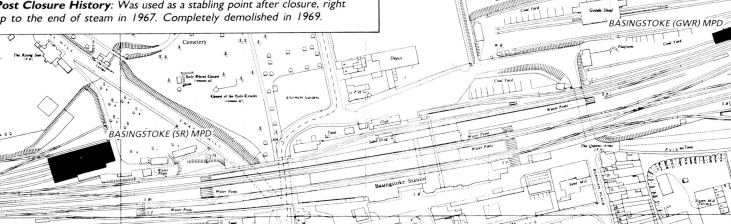

©CROWN COPYRIGHT

**Map Dated:** 1967 (GWR Shed Superimposed)

**Site Location:** North of town centre, adjacent to the A339.

**Track Status:** Basingstoke Station and line are operational.

## 71A(s) LYMINGTON

**Location**: The shed is east of the line, at the north end of Lymington Station.(OS Map Ref; SZ328958)

**Directions**: Entrance to the shed is effected from the station platform.

**Out of Use**: 1966

**Description**: A brick built 1TS through road shed.

*Post Closure History: Demolished, the site is now taken up by a private roadway.*

**LYMINGTON MPD** sited at the north end of the station, photographed on September 29th, 1961.

*WT Stubbs Collection*

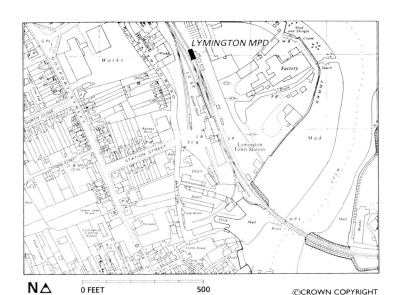

©CROWN COPYRIGHT

**Map Dated:** 1965

**Site Location:** In the north east of the town, on the west bank of the Lymington River and adjacent to the east side of Waterloo Road.

**Track Status:** Lymington Town Station and line are operational.

## 71A(s) ANDOVER JUNCTION

**Location**; The shed is north of the line at the east end of Andover Junction Station. (OS Map Ref; SU356560)

**Directions**; Entrance to the shed is effected from the station platform.

**Out of Use**; 1962

**Description**; A corrugated iron 2TS dead-ended shed sharing the same site as 82C(s) Andover shed.

*Post Closure History*; *Demolished and now site of Industrial Development.*

A quiet moment at **ANDOVER JUNCTION MPD** on September 30th, 1961.
*WT Stubbs Collection*

## 82C(s) ANDOVER

**Location**; The shed is on the north side of the line, at the east end of Andover Junction Station. (OS Map Ref; SU356560)

**Directions**; Entrance to the shed is effected from the station platform.

**Out of Use**; 1958

**Description**; A 2TS timber built dead-ended shed sharing the same site as 71A(s) Andover Junction shed.

*Post Closure History*; *Demolished and now site of Industrial Development.*

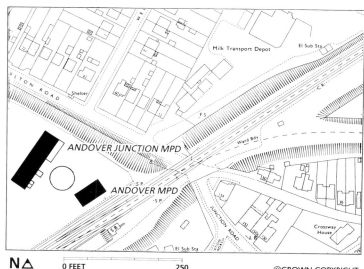

**Map Dated:** 1970 (Shed Superimposed)

**Site Location:** In the north west of the town, on the south side of Charlton Road.

**Track Status:** Andover Station and line are operational.

## 71A EASTLEIGH

**Location**; The shed is on the east side of the Swaythling line, south of Eastleigh Station. (OS Map Ref; SU456181)

**Directions**; Turn left outside the station into the main Southampton Road and turn first left into Campbell Road. Cross the railway bridge and the shed entrance is on the right hand side, a short distance along.

**Closed**; July 1967

**Description**; A brick built 15TS through road shed.

*Post Closure History*; *Demolished. Now a diesel depot (Code EH)*

A distant view of the large **EASTLEIGH MPD** shed building on September 29th, 1961.
*WT Stubbs Collection*

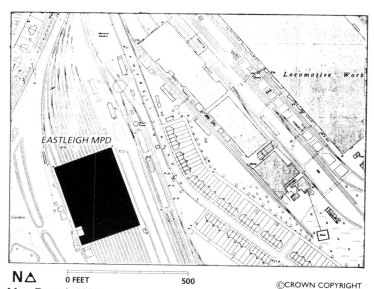

**Map Dated:** 1952

**Site Location:** North of Southampton, adjacent to Southampton Road (A335) and Campbell Road.

**Track Status:** Eastleigh Station and lines are operational.

# 71A(s) WINCHESTER CITY

**Location**: The shed is on a Goods Spur, on the west side of Winchester City Station. (OS Map Ref; SU477300)

**Directions**: Entrance to the shed is effected from the north bound platform.

**Out of Use**: 1963.

**Description**: A corrugated iron ITS through road shed.

**Post Closure History**: *Used as a Stabling Point for a diesel shunter for a few years, but was demolished when the Goods Yard closed in 1969. Now site of Car Park. (1989)*

Ex-LSWR Class B4 0–4–0T No. 30096 occupies the diminutive corrugated iron **WINCHESTER CITY MPD** on September 30th, 1961.
*WT Stubbs Collection*

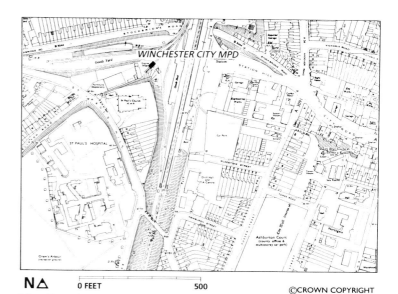

**Map Dated**: 1952

**Site Location**: In the centre of the town, adjacent to the south side of Stockbridge Road (B3044).

**Track Status**: Winchester City Station and line are operational.

# 71E(s) WINCHESTER

**Location**: The shed is east of the line, south of Winchester Chesil Station. (OS Map Ref: SU487288)

**Directions**: Entrance to the shed is effected from the station platform.

**Closed**: July 1953.

**Description**: A stone and brick built ITS through road shed.

**Post Closure History**: *Demolished.*

The site of **WINCHESTER (CHESIL) MPD** photographed on September 30th, 1961.
*WT Stubbs Collection*

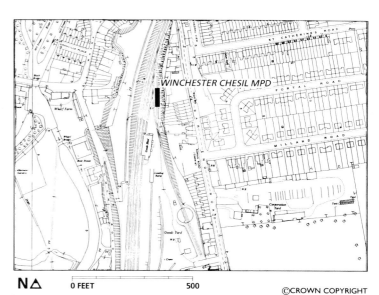

**Map Dated**: 1953

**Site Location**: In the south east of the city, south of East Hill (A272).

**Track Status**: Winchester Chesil Station closed in 1960. Lines lifted.

## 711 SOUTHAMPTON DOCKS

**Location**: The shed is in Southampton Old Docks. (OS Map Ref; SU429105)

**Directions**: Turn sharp left outside of Southampton Terminus Station into Canute Road and enter the Docks by No.7 Gate on the right hand side. Proceed along the Dock Road and upon reaching a number of lines crossing this road turn left and follow the tracks. This leads to the shed.

**Closed**: January 1966 (Steam)

**Description**: A brick built 3TS shed with one through road.

*Post Closure History: Demolished. Site may be redeveloped as part of 'Ocean Village'. (1987)*

**SOUTHAMPTON DOCKS MPD** with its complement of USA Class 0–6–0T locomotives photographed on May 17th, 1953. *John Edgington*

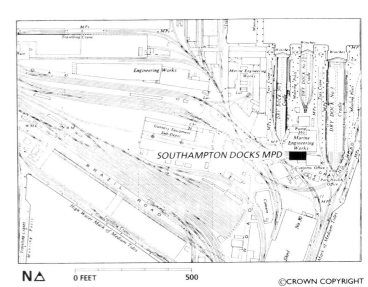

**Map Dated**: 1949

**Site Location:** In the south of the city, south of Canute Road (B3039) and on the west bank of the River Itchen.

## 71A(s) SOUTHAMPTON TERMINUS

**Location**: The shed is north of Southampton Terminus Station, at the end of Western Terrace. (OS Map Ref; SU427113)

**Directions**: Turn right outside of the station along Terminus Terrace, right again into Marsh Lane, and the shed entrance is on the left hand side.

**Closed**: September 5th, 1966

**Description**: Consisting of a Turntable, Water Column, Coaling Stage and some Sidings. There are no Shed Buildings.

*Post Closure History: Demolished. The site is now part of school premises. (1988)*

**Map Dated**: 1949

**Site Location:** In the south of the city, immediately north of Marsh Lane (A33)

**Track Status:** Southampton Terminus Station closed in 1966. Line operational.

## 711(s) SOUTHAMPTON NEW DOCKS

**Location**: The shed is in the New Docks, adjacent to Herbert Walker Avenue. (OS Map Ref; SU397123)

**Directions**: Turn right outside of Southampton Terminus Station along Platform Road, continue along Town Quay and bear left along Herbert Walker Avenue. Enter the docks and the shed is on the right hand side of this road, just before it bends to the right.

**Out of Use**: 1967

**Description**: Consisting of a Turntable and Coaling and Watering Facilities. There are no Shed Buildings.

*Post Closure History: Still intact by 1974. The turntable was sold to GWS for use at Didcot.*

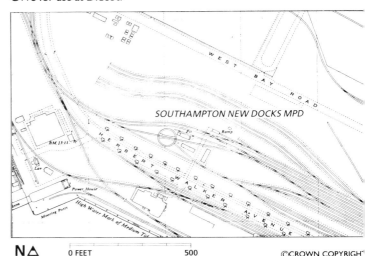

**Map Dated**: 1948

**Site Location:** In the south west of the city, south of Mountbatten Way (A3024).

## 71D(s) GOSPORT

**Location**: The shed is south of the line, west of Gosport Station. (OS Map Ref; SU610001)

**Directions**: Entrance to the shed is effected from the station platform.

**Closed**: June 8th, 1953 and subsequently used as a Stabling Point until 1962.

**Description**: Formerly a brick built 2TS dead ended shed, but after partial demolition in 1953 locomotives stabled in the open.

*Post Closure History: Demolished.*

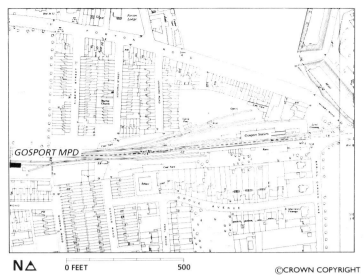

N△    0 FEET    500    ©CROWN COPYRIGHT

**Map Dated:** 1952

**Site Location:** In the centre of the town, south of Forton Road (A32) and immediately north of Kings Road.

**Track Status:** Gosport Station closed in 1953. Lines lifted

The site of **GOSPORT MPD** on September 20th, 1963. The single track remaining had been used as a stabling point until the previous year.

*WT Stubbs Collection*

## 71B BOURNEMOUTH

**Location**: The shed is on the north side of Bournemouth Central Station, at the west end. (OS Map Ref; SZ094921)

**Directions**: The shed entrance is a gate in the yard on the north side of the station.

**Closed**: July 1967.

**Description**: A brick built, asbestos roofed 4TS dead-ended shed.

*Post Closure History: Demolished. The bottom 5ft of the shed wall and the outer and rear lower walls are still intact, forming the boundaries to a Car Park. (1988)*

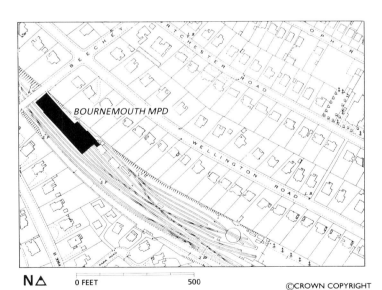

N△    0 FEET    500    ©CROWN COPYRIGHT

**Map Dated:** 1944

**Site Location:** In the centre of the town, adjacent to the junction of the Lansdown Road North (B3064) and Beechey Road.

**Track Status:** Bournemouth Station and line are operational
*The shed was totally demolished in February 1969.*

A view of the yard with **BOURNEMOUTH MPD** in the middle distance taken on September 29th, 1961.

*WT Stubbs Collection*

## 71F RYDE (IOW)

**Location:** The shed is west of the line, at the south end of Ryde St.Johns Road Station. (OS Map Ref; SZ596919)

**Directions:** The shed entrance is in the station yard.

**Closed:** December 31st, 1966.

**Description:** An asbestos built 2TS dead ended shed.

*Post Closure History: Used as a Wagon Shop for a short time. Now demolished, the site is used by a Coal Merchant. (1988)*

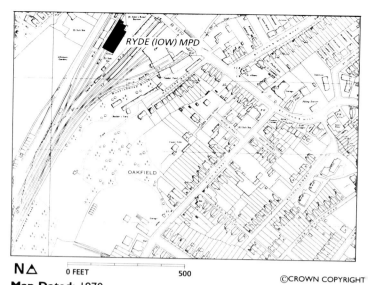

N△    0 FEET    500          ©CROWN COPYRIGHT

**Map Dated:** 1970

**Site Location:** In the south of the town, adjacent to St.John's Hill (B3330).

**Track Status:** Ryde Station and line are operational.

Part of **RYDE MPD**'s stud of Westinghouse Brake fitted Class O2 0–4–4T engines line up on a sunny summer's day. This photograph shows the local practice of painting the stock numbers on the buffer beam in preference to the provision of a cast iron smokebox door number plate.                    *WT Stubbs Collection*

## 71E NEWPORT (IOW)

**Location:** The shed is east of the Cowes line, north of Newport Station. (OS Map Ref; SZ500895)

**Directions:** Entrance to the shed is effected from the station platform.

**Closed:** November 4th, 1957.

**Description:** A corrugated iron 2TS shed with 1 through road.

*Post Closure History: Site partially taken over by a by-pass and traffic island, and partially by a Car Showroom. (1987)*

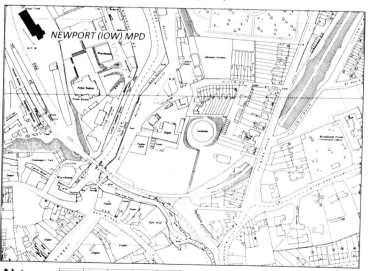

N△    0 FEET    500          ©CROWN COPYRIGHT

**Map Dated:** 1971 (Shed Superimposed)

**Site Location:** In the north of the town, on the west bank of the River Medina and on the north side of Sea Street.

**Track Status:** Newport IOW Station closed in 1966. Lines lifted.

## SITE UTILISATIONS (3)

These days housing estates are built in every nook and cranny and former engine shed sites provide rich pickings for property developers. It is not only common in densely populated urban areas but in rural communities and small towns too. It is difficult to believe that a railway once existed in this view of **HELSTON MPD**, the roadway passing over the shed site in the middle distance, with houses built upon the track bed.                    *Paul Smith*

# PART THREE
# SOUTH EAST ENGLAND

**GREATER LONDON     KENT**
**SURREY          SUSSEX**

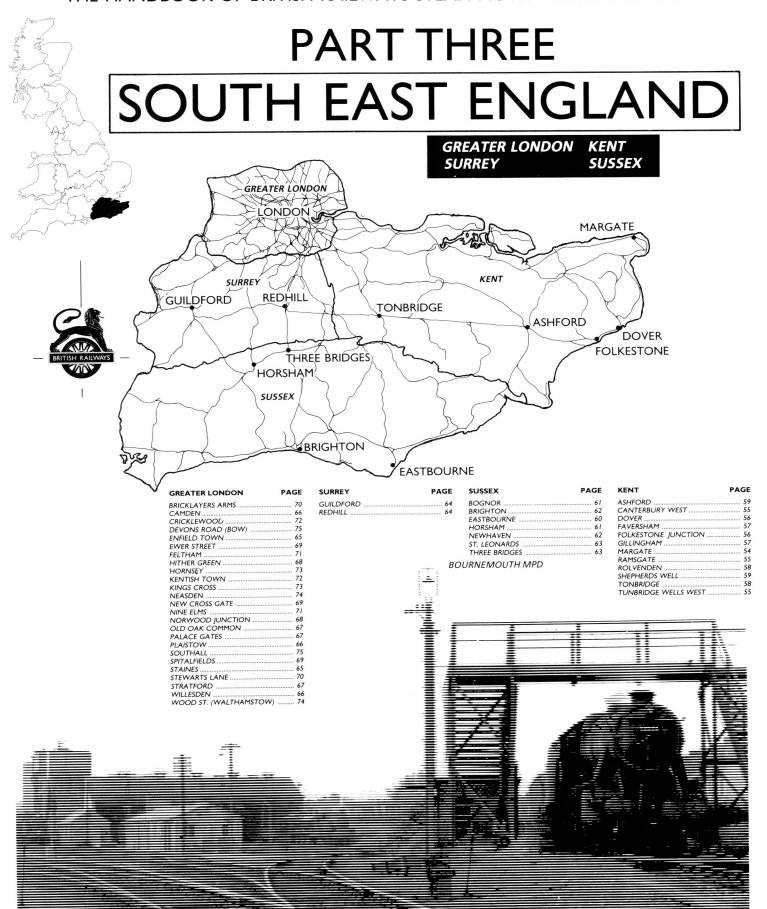

**NORWOOD JUNCTION MPD** *(Lens of Sutton)*

# KENT

## 74A(s) MARGATE

**Location**: The shed is south of the line, at the west end of Margate West Station. (OS Map Ref; TR347705)

**Directions**: Entrance to the shed is effected from the station platform.

**Closed**; June 1961.

**Description**: Consisting of sidings, Engine Pits and a Turntable. There are no shed buildings.

*Post Closure History: Used for stabling emu's for a while. The tracks have been removed and the turntable pit filled in. Part of the site is used as a Coach Park, the remainder is still unused. (1987)*

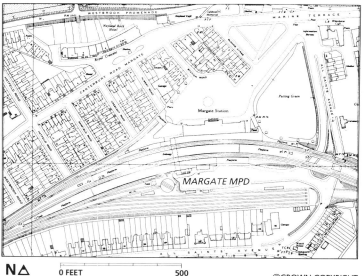

**N△**    0 FEET    500    ©CROWN COPYRIGHT

**Map Dated:** 1955

**Site Location:** In the west of the town, south of Marine Terrace (A28).

**Track Status:** Margate Station and line are operational.

*Originally used only as a turning point for steam locomotives it became a sub shed in its own right upon closure of 74B Ramsgate and until the elimination of steam in the Kent area.*

Diesel locomotives had started to assume ascendency at **MARGATE MPD** when photographed on February 4th, 1961, with steam occupying just two of the tracks available.                                                                      *Sid Nash*

## 75F TUNBRIDGE WELLS WEST

**Location**: The shed is north of the line, at the west end of Tunbridge Wells Station. (OS Map Ref; TQ577384)
**Directions**: The shed entrance is a gate in the Station Yard.
**Closed**: September 9th, 1963.
**Description**: A brick built 4TS dead ended shed.
***Post Closure History****: Still Standing.*

Despite having officially closed some week or so earlier **TUNBRIDGE WELLS WEST MPD** still seemed quite busy servicing tank locomotives on September 21st, 1963.
*WT Stubbs Collection*

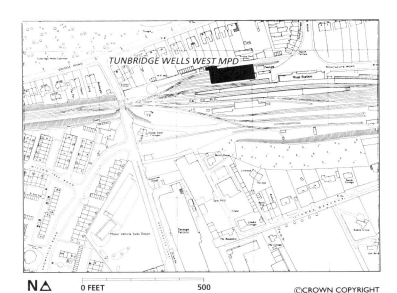

N△  0 FEET  500  ©CROWN COPYRIGHT

**Map Dated:** 1971
**Site Location:** In the south west of the town, adjacent to Eridge Road (A26).
**Track Status:** All lines had been lifted, but during 1989 the Tunbridge Wells & Eridge Railway Preservation Society relaid the shed and shed yard.

## 74B RAMSGATE

**Location**: The shed is north of the line, at the west end of Ramsgate Station. (OS Map Ref; TR375658)
**Directions**: Bear right out of the station approach road into Wilfred Road and turn right into a cinder path following the line. Turn right at the end into Newington Road, cross the bridge and the shed entrance is on the right hand side.
**Closed**: June 1959 (Steam)
**Description**: A 6TS concrete dead ended shed.
***Post Closure History****: The building was extended and is now in use as an emu depot. (Code RE)*

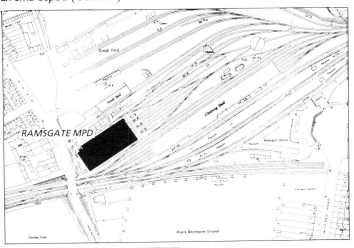

N△  0 FEET  500  ©CROWN COPYRIGHT

**Map Dated:** 1956
**Site Location:** In the north west of the town, north of the A253.
**Track Status:** Ramsgate Station and line are operational.

## 74A(s) CANTERBURY WEST

**Location**: The shed is west of the line, at the north end of Canterbury West Station.  (OS Map Ref; TR146584)
**Directions**: Entrance to the shed is effected from the station platform.
**Closed**: March 1955.
**Description**: A brick built 1TS dead-ended shed.
***Post Closure History****: Demolished. Site Unused.*

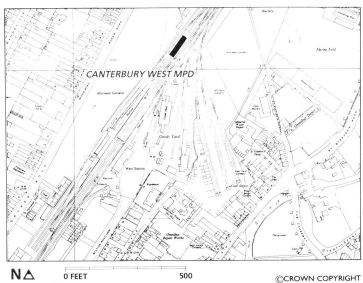

N△  0 FEET  500  ©CROWN COPYRIGHT

**Map Dated:** 1957
**Site Location:** In the north west of the town, Station Road West leads northwards from St.Dunstan's Street (A290).
**Track Status:** Canterbury West Station and line are operational.

## 74C DOVER

**Location**: The shed is on the south side of the line, west of Dover Marine Station. (OS Map Ref; TR317402)

**Directions**: A cinder path leads along the side of the line to the shed from the level crossing, opposite to the entrance to Dover Marine Station.

**Closed**: June 12th, 1961

**Description**: A concrete built 6TS shed with 1 through road.

*Post Closure History: Shed site occupied by sidings. (1987)*

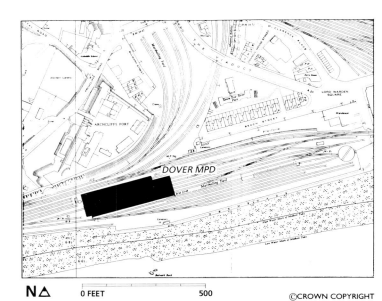

N△   0 FEET   500   ©CROWN COPYRIGHT

**Map Dated:** 1957

**Site Location:** In the south of the town, just west of Western Docks and adjacent to Lord Warden Square.

**Track Status:** Dover Station and lines are operational.

A tired-looking depot, a clinker strewn yard and run down buildings, **DOVER MPD** on February 4th, 1961, four months before closure.     *Sid Nash*

## 74C(s) FOLKESTONE JUNCTION

**Location**: The shed is on the north side of the line, at the east end of Folkestone Junction Station. (OS Map Ref; TR235370)

**Directions**: Entrance to the shed is effected from a gate on the down platform.

**Closed**: June 12th, 1961.

**Description**: A brick built 3TS dead-ended shed.

*Post Closure History: Used as a diesel stabling point for some years, but later demolished (1979)*

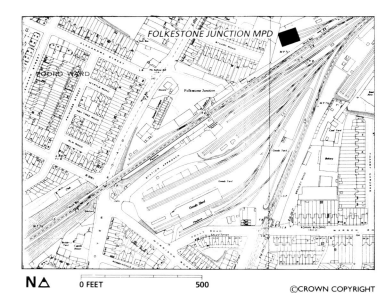

N△   0 FEET   500   ©CROWN COPYRIGHT

**Map Dated:** 1957

**Site Location:** In the north east of the town, adjacent to east side of Dover Road (A2033).

**Track Status:** Folkestone Junction Station closed in 1965. Lines are operational.

Despite two years of closure the tracks were still in situ at **FOLKESTONE JUNCTION MPD** where it housed a goods van on September 23rd, 1963.     *WT Stubbs Collection*

## 73E FAVERSHAM

**Location**: The shed is in the fork of the Margate and Canterbury lines, east of Faversham Station. (OS Map Ref; TQ020608)

**Directions**: Turn right outside of the station along Station Road, left into St. Mary's Road and right into Chapel Street. Cross the park at the end of this street and ascend a flight of steps. These steps lead to a footbridge across the railway line. The shed entrance is at the bottom of a flight of steps at the centre of this bridge.

**Closed**: June 1959

**Description**: A brick built 4TS dead ended shed.

*Post Closure History: Still standing, totally intact, it is now the subject of a preservation order.(1988)*

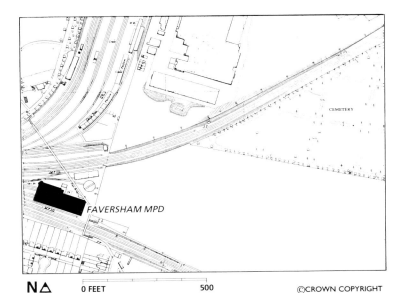

N△   0 FEET   500   ©CROWN COPYRIGHT

**Map Dated:** 1962
**Site Location:** In the south of the town, just north of London Road (A2)
**Track Status:** Faversham Station and lines are operational.

Photographed on September 24th, 1963 the fuel tanks in the shed yard at **FAVERSHAM MPD** reveal its role as a major diesel stabling point following closure to steam in 1959.          *WT Stubbs Collection*

## 73D GILLINGHAM (KENT)

**Location**: The shed is south of the line, east of Gillingham Station.(OS Map Ref; TQ779684)

**Directions**: Turn left outside of the station, first left into Balmoral Road, first left again into Avondale Road and bear right into Windsor Road. A paved pathway leads from the left hand side to the shed.

**Closed**: June 13th, 1960.

**Description**: A brick built 3TS shed with 2 through roads.

*Post Closure History: Demolished. Site of Industrial development (1972)*

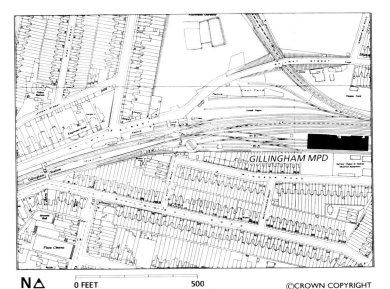

N△   0 FEET   500   ©CROWN COPYRIGHT

**Map Dated:** 1955
**Site Location:** In the centre of the town, north of Windsor Road.
**Track Status:** Gillingham Station and line are operational.

A derelict **GILLINGHAM MPD** on September 24th, 1963.
                                  *WT Stubbs Collection*

## 74A(s) ROLVENDEN

**Location**: The shed is west of the line, at the north end of Rolvenden Station. (OS Map Ref; TQ864328)

**Directions**: Entrance to the shed is effected from the station platform.

**Closed**: January 1954.

**Description**: A corrugated asbestos and wooden 2TS dead ended shed.

***Post Closure History***: *Demolished. The site is part of the K&ESR Preservation Group's Headquarters.*

**ROLVENDEN MPD** in private use on September 21st, 1963.

*WT Stubbs Collection*

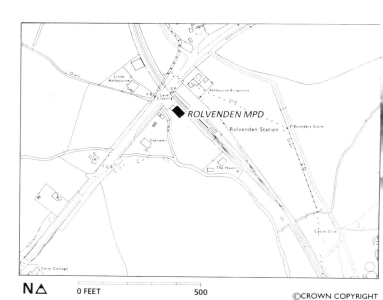

N△   0 FEET   500                    ©CROWN COPYRIGHT

**Map Dated:** 1973 (Shed Superimposed)

**Site Location:** Adjacent to the A28 about one mile west of Tenterden.

**Track Status:** Rolvenden Station is now part of the preserved Kent and East Sussex Railway which re-opened on February 3rd, 1974.

## 74D TONBRIDGE

**Location**: The shed is in the fork of the Ashford and Tunbridge Wells lines, at the east end of Tonbridge Station. (OS Map Ref; TQ591459)

**Directions**: Leave the station by the main exit, turn right over the bridge, left into Priory Road and the shed entrance is a gate on the left hand side.

**Closed**: June 1964.

**Description**: A brick built 6TS shed with 4 through roads.

***Post Closure History***: *Demolished. Offices still standing. Remainder of site used for stabling diesel locomotives. (1987)*

The spectre of impending dieselisation hangs heavily over **TONBRIDGE MPD** on September 21st, 1963 as a Class 33 diesel locomotive ticks over alongside the fuelling point. Nine months later the depot closed to steam.

*WT Stubbs Collection*

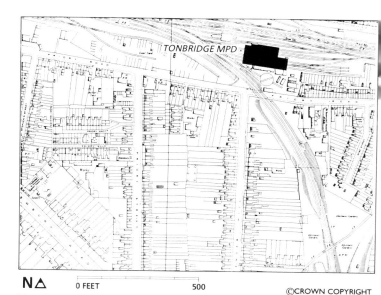

N△   0 FEET   500                    ©CROWN COPYRIGHT

**Map Dated:** 1960

**Site Location:** South of the town centre, on the east side of Quarry Hill Road (A26) and immediately north of Priory Road.

**Track Status:** Tonbridge Station and lines are operational.

## 74A ASHFORD (KENT)

**Location**: The shed is on the east side of the Folkestone line, south of Ashford Station. (OS Map Ref; TR022417)

**Directions**: Leave the station by the main exit and at the end of the approach road turn left over the railway bridge. Turn left again down a road at the end of this bridge and follow it for about a mile, passing the entrance to the works. At the end of the works site turn left over a level crossing and a broad path leads to the shed from the left hand side of the road a short distance along.

**Closed**: June 1962 (Steam), 1968 (Totally)

**Description**: A concrete 10TS dead-ended shed.

**Post Closure History**: *Following closure it was used as the home for the South Eastern Steam Centre, a preservation group, but since they vacated it the whole shed is now in a derelict condition, with all lines lifted and the shed yard is now a wilderness. The site is currently in use for motor vehicle storage. (1988)*

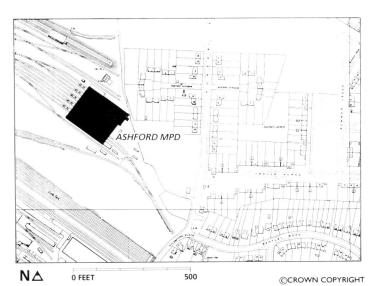

N△    0 FEET    500    ©CROWN COPYRIGHT

**Map Dated**: 1960

**Site Location**: South east of the town centre, on the west side of Hunter Avenue.

**Track Status**: Ashford Station and lines are operational

◄A totally dieselised **ASHFORD MPD** on September 22nd, 1963.
*WT Stubbs Collection*

## 74C(s) SHEPHERDS WELL

**Location**: The shed is north of the Sandwich line, at the east end of Shepherds Well (EKR) Station. (OS Map Ref; TR257483)

**Directions**: Entrance to the shed is effected from the station platform.

**Closed**: November 1948.

**Description**: A corrugated asbestos and wooden 2TS dead ended shed.

**Post Closure History**: *Demolished. Site unused.*

**SHEPHERDS WELL MPD** on September 4th, 1948 with Class O1 Locomotive EKR No. 2 (BR No. 31383) shunting stock into the station for the evening train to Wingham.
*Sid Nash*

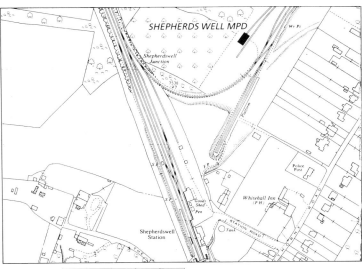

N△    0 FEET    500    ©CROWN COPYRIGHT

**Map Dated**: 1957

**Site Location**: In the north of the village, on the west side of Eythorne Road.

**Track Status**: Shepherds Well (SR) Station and line are operational. Shepherds Well (EKR) Station closed in 1948, the line was used for mineral traffic only until at least 1974.

# SUSSEX

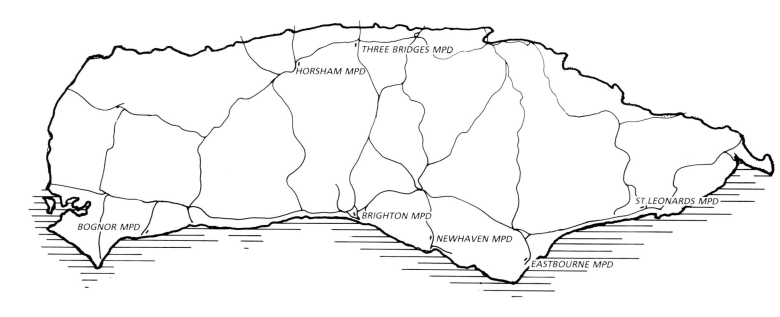

## 75G EASTBOURNE

**Location**; The shed is on the west side of the line, about 1 mile north of Eastbourne Station. (OS Map Ref; TQ613000)

**Directions**; Turn right outside of the station along Station Parade, turn right into The Avenue and bear right into Upper Avenue. After a few yards take the left hand fork and continue into Corringe Road. A broad cinder path leads through the allotments on the right hand side to the shed.

**Out of Use**; c1968

**Description**; A 7TS brick built through road shed.

*Post Closure History; Demolished in 1969. Site Unused (1980)*

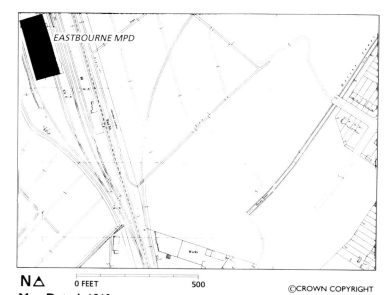

N△   0 FEET          500          ©CROWN COPYRIGHT

**Map Dated:** 1960

**Site Location:** In the north of the town

**Track Status:** Eastbourne Station and line are operational.

A brand new Nine Elms allocated Britannia Class 4–6–2 No. 70009 *ALFRED THE GREAT* checks into **EASTBOURNE MPD** on June 3rd, 1951.          *Sid Nash*

## 75D HORSHAM

**Location**: The shed is east of the line, north of Horsham Station.(OS Map Ref; TQ 180314)

**Directions**: Turn right out of the station, cross the bridge, turn left into Foundry Road and a cinder path leads to the shed from a gate on the left hand side.

**Closed**: July 18th, 1959 (Steam), June 15th, 1964 (Totally)

**Description**: A brick built 18 stall open type Roundhouse.

***Post Closure History***: *The site has been given over to Industrial Development.*

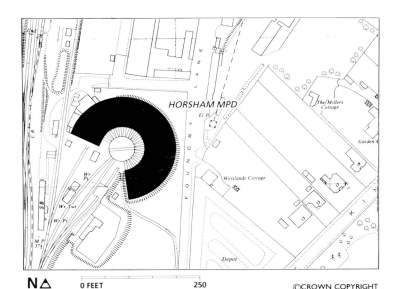

Map Dated: 1964
**Site Location:** In the town centre, adjacent to the north side of the A264.
**Track Status:** Horsham Station and line are operational.

The open semi-roundhouse at **HORSHAM MPD**, photographed on September 21st, 1963 and still servicing steam locomotives, despite being closed to steam in 1959.                                        *WT Stubbs Collection*

## 75D(s) BOGNOR

**Location**: The shed is east of the line, at the north end of Bognor Regis Station.  (OS Map Ref; TL935996)

**Directions**: Entrance to the shed is effected from the station platform.

**Out of Use**: 1953

**Description**: A brick built 2TS through road shed.

***Post Closure History****: Most of the shed has been demolished, but the offices in the east wall still remain (1979)*

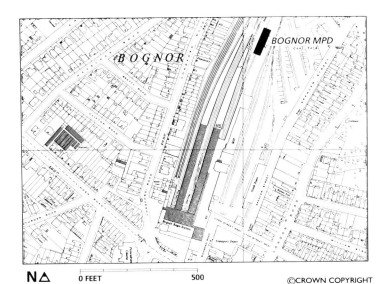

Map Dated: 1963 (Shed Superimposed)
**Site Location:** In the town centre, the station is adjacent to Station Road (A29)
**Track Status:** Bognor Regis Station and line are operational.
*The locomotive accomodation part of the shed buildings was demolished in 1956.*

The remains of **BOGNOR REGIS MPD** on September 20th, 1963. The turntable, water tower, offices and one road with engine pit were all still in situ and in use.                                        *WT Stubbs Collection*

## 75A BRIGHTON

**Location**: The shed is in the fork of the Haywards Heath and Worthing lines at the north end of Brighton Station. (OS Map Ref; TQ308053)

**Directions**: Turn right outside of the station along Terminus Road and continue into Howard Place. Turn right into New England Road and a broad path leads from the right hand side to the shed.

**Closed**: June 15th, 1964.

**Description**: A brick built 14TS dead-ended shed.

*Post Closure History*: *Demolished. The site is occupied by a freight depot.*

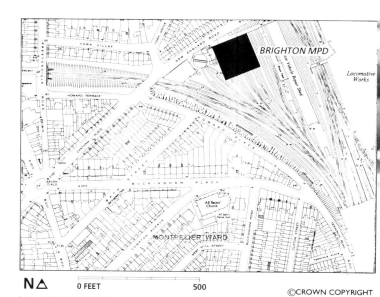

N△    0 FEET    500    ©CROWN COPYRIGHT

**Map Dated:** 1953

**Site Location:** Just north of the town centre, adjacent to the junction of Howard Place (A2010) and New England Road (B2122)

**Track Status:** Brighton Station and line are operational.

A mixed bag of locomotives were present at **BRIGHTON MPD** when photographed on September 22nd, 1963.                    *WT Stubbs Collection*

## 75A(s) NEWHAVEN

**Location**: The shed is on the west side of Newhaven Station. (OS Map Ref; TQ448014)

**Directions**: A cinder path leads from the north end of the westernmost platform to the shed.

**Closed**: September 9th, 1963.

**Description**: A corrugated iron 4TS dead ended shed.

*Post Closure History*: *Still Standing, in industrial use (1988)*

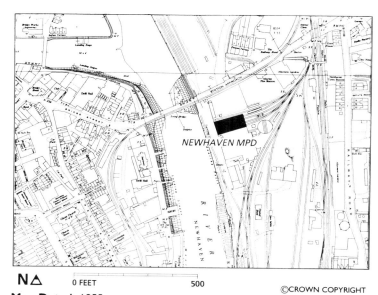

N△    0 FEET    500    ©CROWN COPYRIGHT

**Map Dated:** 1955

**Site Location:** On the east bank of the River Ouse, adjacent to the south side of Station Approach (A259).

**Track Status:** Newhaven Town Station and line are operational.

A deserted **NEWHAVEN MPD** on September 22nd, 1963, just a fortnight after closure.                    *WT Stubbs Collection*

# 74E ST.LEONARDS

**Location**: The shed is on the north side of St.Leonards West Marina Station. (OS Map Ref; TQ787089)

**Directions**: A gate on the eastbound platform leads to the shed.

**Closed**: June 1958.

**Description**: A brick built 4TS through road shed.

*Post Closure History: Demolished.*

Although closed some five years previously a very much intact **ST.LEONARDS MPD** was in use for wagon storage and as a diesel stabling point when photographed on September 22nd, 1963. *WT Stubbs Collection*

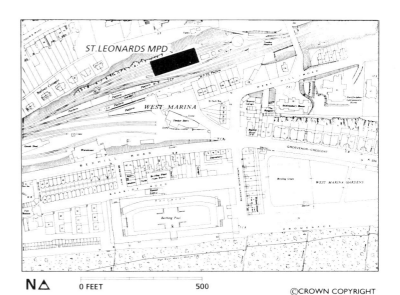

N△     0 FEET     500     ©CROWN COPYRIGHT

**Map Dated:** 1955

**Site Location:** In the west of St.Leonards, just north of Bexhill Road (A259).

**Track Status:** St.Leonards West Marina Station closed in 1967. Lines are operational.

# 75E THREE BRIDGES

**Location**: The shed is in the fork of the Haywards Heath and Horsham lines, south of Three Bridges Station. (OS Map Ref; TQ286364)

**Directions**: Go straight ahead out of the station, turn left along the main road and left again along a cinder path (alongside an electricity substation). This leads under the Horsham line, to the shed.

**Closed**: June 1964

**Description**: A brick built 3TS through road shed.

*Post Closure History: Demolished 1974. Now site of Engineers Yard. (1988)*

Steam and diesel locomotives share the premises at **THREE BRIDGES MPD** on September 21st, 1963. *WT Stubbs Collection*

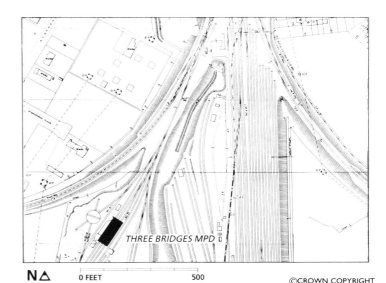

N△     0 FEET     500     ©CROWN COPYRIGHT

**Map Dated:** 1961

**Site Location:** East of Crawley, south of Three Bridges Road (A264).

**Track Status:** Three Bridges Station and lines are operational

# SURREY

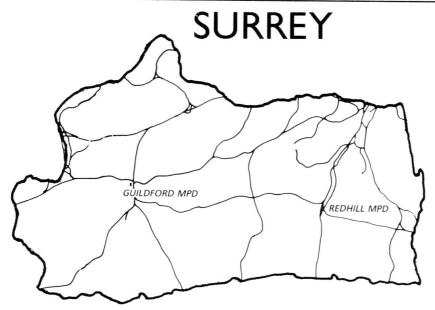

## 75B REDHILL

**Location**: The shed is in the fork of the Brighton and Tonbridge lines, south of Redhill Station. (OS Map Ref; TQ281501)

**Directions**: Turn left outside of the main entrance on the northbound side, left again under the bridge along Station Road, bear right and a Private Road on the right hand side leads to the shed through the Goods Yard.

**Closed**: January 4th, 1965.

**Description**: A brick built 3TS through road shed.

**Post Closure History**: *Partially Demolished, the offices are still standing. The site is now used for servicing diesel locomotives. (1988)*

**REDHILL MPD** on September 21st, 1963.          *WT Stubbs Collection*

## 70C GUILDFORD

**Location**: The shed is on the west side of the line, south of Guildford Station. (OS Map Ref; TQ997494)

**Directions**: Turn right outside the station and first right into Farnham Road. The shed entrance is on the left hand side, just past the railway bridge.

**Closed**: July 9th, 1967.

**Description**: A brick built open-type semi-circular roundhouse and 4TS shed.

**Post Closure History**: *Demolished in April 1969. The site was utilised as a car park until 1988. Currently being redeveloped (1988)*

The unusual layout of **GUILDFORD MPD**, photographed in 1958, consisted of a semi-roundhouse with some of the roads running parallel to the line being extended to form an extra straighthouse.          *Peter Winding*

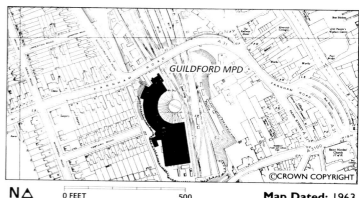

N△   0 FEET          500          **Map Dated:** 1966

N△   0 FEET          500          **Map Dated:** 1963

# GREATER LONDON

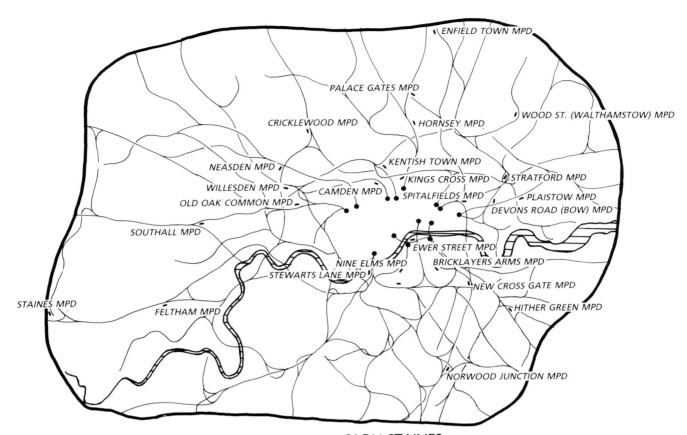

Map labels:
ENFIELD TOWN MPD · PALACE GATES MPD · WOOD ST. (WALTHAMSTOW) MPD · CRICKLEWOOD MPD · HORNSEY MPD · KENTISH TOWN MPD · NEASDEN MPD · KINGS CROSS MPD · STRATFORD MPD · WILLESDEN MPD · CAMDEN MPD · SPITALFIELDS MPD · PLAISTOW MPD · OLD OAK COMMON MPD · DEVONS ROAD (BOW) MPD · SOUTHALL MPD · EWER STREET MPD · NINE ELMS MPD · BRICKLAYERS ARMS MPD · STEWARTS LANE MPD · NEW CROSS GATE MPD · STAINES MPD · FELTHAM MPD · HITHER GREEN MPD · NORWOOD JUNCTION MPD

## 30A(s) ENFIELD TOWN

**Location**; The shed is on the west side of Enfield Town Station. (OS Map Ref; TQ330965)

**Directions**; A path leads along the side of the line from the station entrance to the shed.

**Closed**: November 30th, 1960

**Description**; A brick built 1TS through road shed

*Post Closure History: Demolished.*

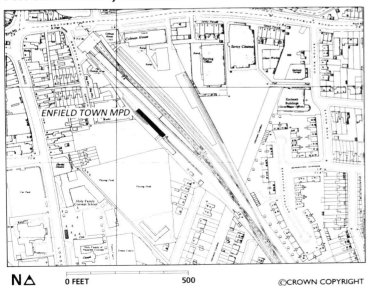

N△  0 FEET  500  ©CROWN COPYRIGHT

**Map Dated:** 1956

**Site Location:** In the town centre, adjacent to the south side of Southbury Road (A110)

**Track Status:** Enfield Town Station and line are operational

## 81C(s) STAINES

**Location**; The shed is west of the line, at the north end of Staines Station. (OS Map Ref; TQ033720)

**Directions**: Entrance to the shed is effected from the station platform.

**Closed**: June 1952.

**Description**: Formerly a wooden 1TS shed, but latterly consisted of just an Engine Pit and Water Column.

*Post Closure History: Demolished.*

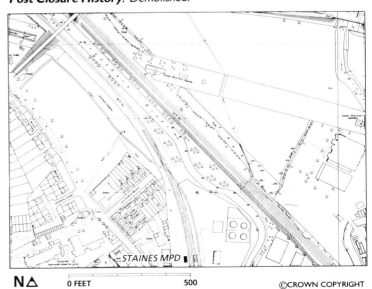

N△  0 FEET  500  ©CROWN COPYRIGHT

**Map Dated:** 1972 (Shed Superimposed)

**Site Location:** South West of London, in the west of the town.

**Track Status:** Staines (GW) Station closed in 1965. Lines lifted.

## 33A PLAISTOW

**Location**: The shed is south of the line, midway between West Ham and Plaistow Stations. (OS Map Ref; TQ396830)

**Directions**: Turn left outside of West Ham (District Line) Station into Manor Lane, left into Memorial Avenue and left at the end into Springfield Road. Turn right into Holland Road and the shed entrance is at the end of this road.

**Closed**: November 2nd, 1959 (Steam): June 18th, 1962 (Totally).

**Description**: A brick built 8TS dead ended shed.

*Post Closure History: Demolished. Now site of 'East London Rugby Club' Playing Fields. (1988)*

Despite being officially closed to steam some years earlier **PLAISTOW MPD** still appears to have a healthy collection of locomotives on September 18th, 1960.
*WT Stubbs Collection*

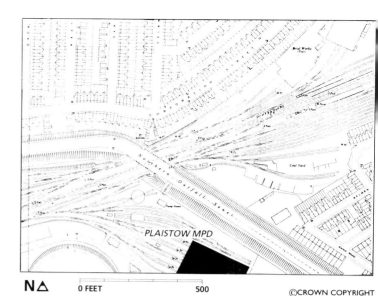

N△    0 FEET    500    ©CROWN COPYRIGHT

**Map Dated:** 1951

**Site Location:** East London. Adjacent to the south side of the Northern Outfall Sewer and immediately north of East London Cemetery.

**Track Status:** Lines are operational.

## 1A WILLESDEN

**Location**: The shed is west of the main line, north of Willesden Junction. (OS Map Ref; TQ213829)

**Directions**: Leave Willesden Junction (BR & LT) Station by the approach road, turn left into Old Oak Lane, right into Goodhall Street and a path leads from the end to the shed.

**Closed**: September 27th, 1965.

**Description**: A large depot complex consisting of a brick built round-house and a brick built 12TS dead ended shed.

*Post Closure History: Demolished. Now site of Freightliner Depot.*

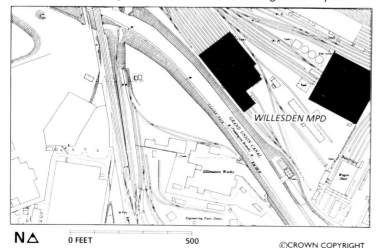

N△    0 FEET    500    ©CROWN COPYRIGHT

**Map Dated:** 1955

**Site Location:** North West London. Immediately north of the Grand Union Canal, south of Harlesden.

**Track Status:** Willesden Junction Station and lines are operational.
*The shed was demolished in December 1966.*

## 1B CAMDEN

**Location**: The shed is on the west side of the West Coast Main line about 1.5 miles north of Euston Station. (OS Map Ref; TQ283842)

**Directions**: Leave Chalk Farm (Northern Line) Station by the Adelaide Road exit and turn right. Turn first left into Bridge Approach and continue into Regents Park Road, cross the railway bridge and turn left into Gloucester Avenue. Turn left into Dumpton Place and the shed entrance is a gate in the wall at the end of this cul-de-sac.

**Closed**: September 9th, 1963 (Steam), January 3rd, 1966 (Totally)

**Description**: A brick built 5TS through road shed.

*Post Closure History: Demolished, the site is now occupied by sidings.*

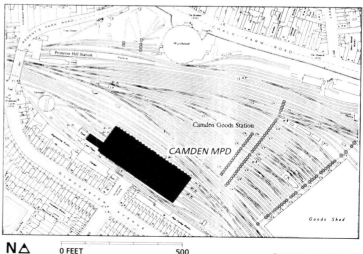

N△    0 FEET    500    ©CROWN COPYRIGHT

**Map Dated:** 1955

**Site Location:** North Central London. South of the Chalk Farm Road (A502).

## 30A STRATFORD

**Location**: The shed is amongst a maze of lines on the north west side of Stratford Station. (OS Map Ref; TQ383848)

**Directions**: Turn right out of the station entrance and a tunnel runs under the railway, from William Street, to the shed.

**Closed**: September 1962 (Steam)

**Description**: The depot was an integral part of the Stratford Works site and was basically composed of a brick built 6TS through road 'New' shed and a brick built 12TS through road 'Jubilee' shed.

**Post Closure History**: *Most of the steam running shed buildings have been demolished and replaced by a purpose built diesel depot (Code SF).*

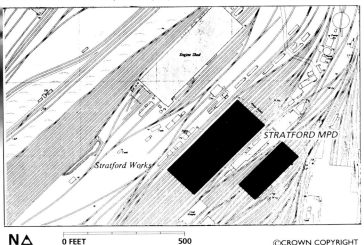

N△  0 FEET        500        ©CROWN COPYRIGHT

**Map Dated:** 1951
**Site Location:** East London. North of High Street (A11).
**Track Status:** All lines operational.
*The last part of the steam depot was demolished in 1984.*

## 81A OLD OAK COMMON

**Location**: The shed is on the north side of the junction of the Reading and High Wycombe lines, 2 miles west of Westbourne Park Station.(OS Map Ref; TQ216823)

**Directions**: Leave Willesden Junction (LMR and LT) Station by means of the approach road, turn left into Old Oak Lane and left again into Old Oak Common Lane. A drive leads to the shed from the left hand side.

**Closed**: March 22nd, 1965 (Steam)

**Description**: A large brick built four roundhouse shed.

**Post Closure History**: *Most of the shed buildings have been demolished and replaced by a purpose built Diesel Depot (Code OC).*

A general view of the depot buildings at **OLD OAK COMMON**, photographed on July 3rd, 1963.
*WT Stubbs Collection*

## 30A(s) PALACE GATES

**Location**: The shed is east of the line, north of Palace Gates Station.(OS Map Ref; TQ302909)

**Directions**: From Bounds Green (LT) Station: Turn left along Bounds Green Road, right into Imperial Road and the shed entrance is at the end.

**Out of Use**: 1954

**Description**: A brick built 2TS dead ended shed.

**Post Closure History**: *Demolished. Part of the shed site is incorporated into Bounds Green HST Depot sidings. (1988)*

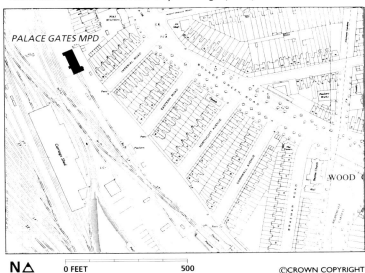

N△  0 FEET        500        ©CROWN COPYRIGHT

**Map Dated:** 1956
**Site Location:** North London. South of North Circular Road (A406) and west of Bounds Green Road.
**Track Status:** Palace Gates Station closed in 1963. Lines lifted.

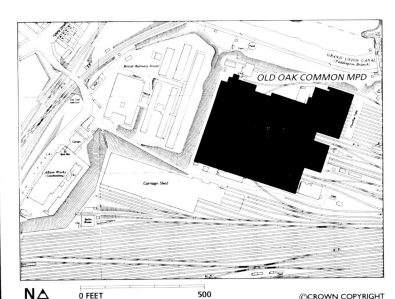

N△  0 FEET        500        ©CROWN COPYRIGHT

**Map Dated:** 1955
**Site Location:** West London. South of the Grand Union Canal, north of Westway (A40).
**Track Status:** Lines are operational.

## 75C NORWOOD JUNCTION

**Location**: The shed is east of the Anerley line, north of Norwood Junction Station. (OS Map Ref; TQ343690)

**Directions**: Leave the station by the main entrance, turn right along a footpath, left at the end into Portland Road, right into High Street and proceed over a railway bridge into Penge Road. A cinder path leads over a footbridge to the shed from the left hand side.

**Closed**: June 5th, 1964.

**Description**: A concrete built 5TS dead ended shed.

*Post Closure History: Demolished. Now site of CMEE's Cable depot. (1988)*

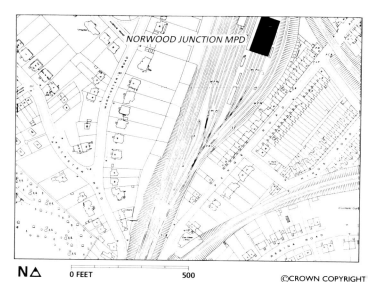

NΔ  0 FEET  500  ©CROWN COPYRIGHT

**Map Dated:** 1954

**Site Location:** South London. West of the Penge Road (A213) and south of Penge.

**Track Status:** Norwood Junction Station and lines are operational.

**NORWOOD JUNCTION MPD** viewed from the footbridge.

*Lens of Sutton*

## 73C HITHER GREEN

**Location**: The shed is in the triangle of the Hither Green to Dartford to Tonbridge lines. (OS Map Ref; TQ392742)

**Directions**: A cinder path leads from No.4 Platform to the shed.

**Closed**: October 1961 (Steam)

**Description**: A concrete 6TS dead ended shed.

*Post Closure History: In use as a diesel depot (Code HG) until closure on November 24th, 1985 and subsequently as a Stabling Point (1988)*

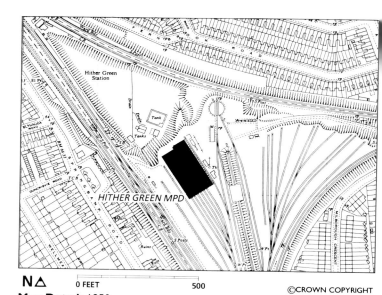

NΔ  0 FEET  500  ©CROWN COPYRIGHT

**Map Dated:** 1950

**Site Location:** South East London. North of the Brownhill Road (A205 South Circular Road) and immediately west of Milborough Crescent.

**Track Status:** Hither Green Station and lines are operational.

*\*\* Due to re-open as a Freight Sector depot for the servicing of Class 60 locomotives*

A pre-dieselisation view of **HITHER GREEN MPD** taken in June 1960.

*Photomatic*

## 73B(s) EWER STREET

**Location**: The shed is north of the Blackfriars to London Bridge line, west of London Bridge Station. (OS Map Ref; TQ320801)

**Directions**: From Waterloo Station; Leave by the eastern exit, turn left into Bayliss Road, cross Waterloo Road and proceed along The Cut. Continue into Union Street and turn first left into Gambia Street. At the end of this street, at the junction with Dolben Street, there is an entrance to the Goods Depot on the right hand side. Enter the depot and follow the drive up the hill. The depot is at the end of this drive.

**Out of Use**: 1961

**Description**: Consisting of a turntable and basic servicing facilities. There are no shed buildings.

***Post Closure History***: *The site was partially used for emu stabling, but has since been abandoned. Site Unused. (1988)*

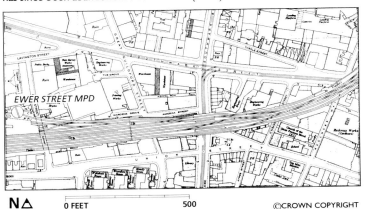

N△     0 FEET     500     ©CROWN COPYRIGHT

**Map Dated**: 1953

**Site Location**: South East London. On the corner of Ewer Street and Union Street.

**Track Status**: The lines are operational.

## 73B(s) NEW CROSS GATE

**Location**: The shed is west of the line, at the north end of New Cross Gate Station. (OS Map Ref; TQ361770)

**Directions**: Turn right outside of the station, right again and the shed entrance is at the end of this road.

**Closed**: May 23rd, 1949 and used as a Stabling Point until 1951.

**Description**: A cramped layout consisting of a brick built roundhouse, two 3TS dead ended sheds and a 4TS through road shed.

***Post Closure History***: *All the buildings were in a very dilapidated condition due to war damage and were finally demolished in 1957.*

The 'Croydon' shed at **NEW CROSS GATE MPD** was in a fine state of decrepitude and offering little protection from the elements for men and machines when photographed just prior to nationalisation. Pencilled in for closure in the 1930s the events of World War 2 both extended its existence into BR days as an operating necessity and assisted in its demolition.

*Lens of Sutton*

## 30A(s) SPITALFIELDS

**Location**: The shed is in the fork of the Liverpool to Stratford and Shoreditch lines. (OS Map Ref; TQ345823)

**Directions**: Entrance to the shed is effected by a pathway alongside of the up line from the westbound side of Bethnal Green Station.

**Out of Use**: 1960

**Description**: A brick built 1TS dead ended shed.

***Post Closure History***: *Demolished. Site Unused.*

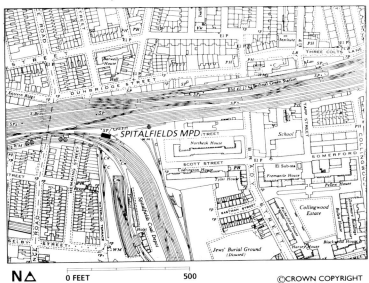

N△     0 FEET     500     ©CROWN COPYRIGHT

**Map Dated**: 1951

**Site Location**: East London. Immediately south of Dunbridge Street.

**Track Status**: Bethnal Green Station and lines are operational.

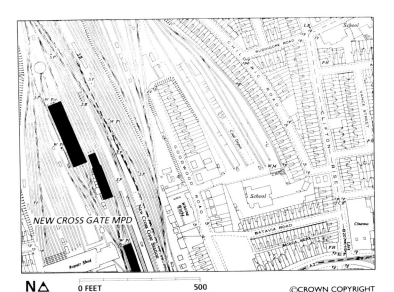

N△     0 FEET     500     ©CROWN COPYRIGHT

**Map Dated**: 1952

**Site Location**: South East London. Adjacent to the north side of the New Cross Road (A2).

**Track Status**: New Cross Gate Station and line are operational.

*The buildings, reading from north to south, were known as 'New Shed', 'Middle Shed' and 'Croydon Shed'*

## 73A STEWARTS LANE

**Location**: The shed is amongst a maze of lines, between Wandsworth Road and Battersea Park Stations. (OS Map Ref; TQ290765)

**Directions**: Turn left out of Queens Road (Battersea) Station into Queenstown Road, fork left into Silverthorne Road and the shed entrance is a gate on the left hand side marked 'Longhedge Works'

**Closed**: September 1963 (Steam)

**Description**: A brick built 16TS dead ended shed.

*Post Closure History: Used as a diesel and electric depot (Code SL)*

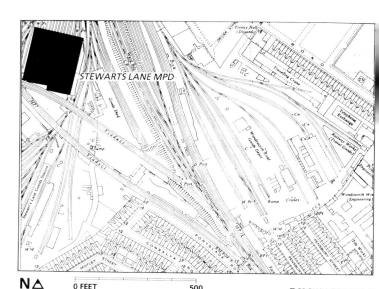

**N△** 0 FEET 500 ©CROWN COPYRIGHT

**Map Dated:** 1952

**Site Location:** South London. North of Wandsworth Road (B3036) and west of Stewarts Road.

**Track Status:** Lines operational.

A cosmopolitan collection of rolling stock is visible in this 1960s view of **STEWARTS LANE MPD**. The corrugated front to the northern patternlight roof was an unusual feature of this depot building.

*Lens of Sutton*

## 73B BRICKLAYERS ARMS

**Location**: The shed is in the Bricklayers Arms Goods Yard, at the end of a spur. (OS Map Ref; TQ335787)

**Directions**: Proceed along New Kent Road from outside of the Elephant & Castle Underground Station. Turn right into Old Kent Road and the entrance to the Goods Yard, on the left at the junction with Pages Walk, is a cobbled road. This leads to the shed

**Closed**: June 18th, 1962.

**Description**: Composed of a brick built 4TS dead ended shed and a brick built 8TS shed with 5 through roads. A large repair shop occupies the rear of the site.

*Post Closure History: The site is now being developed as an Industrial Estate, although by as late as 1987 the Works and two side walls of one of the running sheds were still standing.*

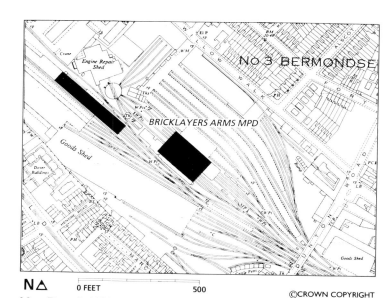

**N△** 0 FEET 500 ©CROWN COPYRIGHT

**Map Dated:** 1952

**Site Location:** South Central London, adjacent to the junction of Old Kent Road (A2) and Dunton Road (B203)

The eight track straighthouse at **BRICKLAYERS ARMS MPD**, photographed on September 18th, 1960.

*WT Stubbs Collection*

## 70A NINE ELMS

**Location**: The shed is on a spur off the main line between Vauxhall and Queens Road Stations. (OS Map Ref; TQ296770)

**Directions**: Turn right outside of Wandsworth Road Station along Wandsworth Road, left into Brooklands Road and the shed entrance is at the end.

**Closed**: July 9th, 1967

**Description**: Originally composed of 2 brick built dead ended structures, the 15TS 'old' shed and 10 TS 'new' shed. Most of the roof cover had gone by closure.

**Post Closure History**: *Demolished. Now site of Nine Elms Fruit and Vegetable Market. (1988)*

Part of the sprawling shed complex at **NINE ELMS MPD**. Although photographed on July 16th, 1967, only one week after closure, it has the appearance of near total dereliction.                  *WT Stubbs Collection*

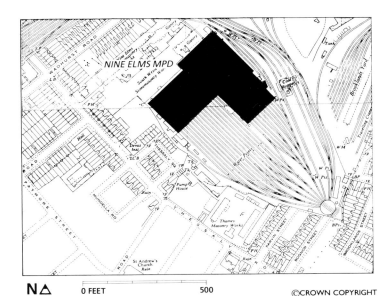

N△        0 FEET          500          ©CROWN COPYRIGHT

**Map Dated:** 1952
**Site Location:** South London. On the north side of Thessaly Road, west of Wandsworth Road (B3036).
**Track Status:** Lines operational.
*The shed was demolished in 1968*

## 70B FELTHAM

**Location**: The shed is south of the line, east of Feltham Station.(OS Map Ref; TQ123736)

**Directions**: Go straight ahead outside Hounslow Station along Station Road, turn left into Hanworth Road and after about a mile a drive leads to the shed from the right hand side, opposite the junction of Powder Mill Lane.

**Closed**: July 1967

**Description**: A concrete built 6TS through road shed.

**Post Closure History**: *Demolished. Site Unused. (1988)*

A tatty looking **FELTHAM MPD** on September 25th, 1963.
                                            *WT Stubbs Collection*

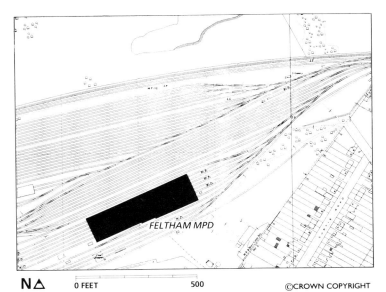

N△        0 FEET          500          ©CROWN COPYRIGHT

**Map Dated:** 1962
**Site Location:** South West London. West of Hanworth Road (A314), south of Hounslow.
**Track Status:** Marshalling yards lifted, line operational.
*The shed closed completely in August 1970.*

## 14A CRICKLEWOOD

**Location**: The shed is on the west side of the main line, north of Cricklewood Station. (OS Map Ref; TQ232867)

**Directions**: Turn right outside of the station along Cricklewood Lane and right into Edgeware Road. Proceed under the first railway bridge, and over the second, and the shed entrance is on the right hand side at the end of the shed buildings.

**Closed**: December 14th, 1964.

**Description**: A brick built double-roundhouse.

**Post Closure History**: *Demolished, although the repair shop still stands in industrial use. (1988)*

N△  0 FEET  500   ©CROWN COPYRIGHT

**Map Dated**: 1955

**Site Location**: North West London. Just south of the junction of the M1 and A406 roads, adjacent to the east side of Edgeware Road (A5).

**Track Status**: The lines are operational.

The depot closed completely in 1967 and was demolished two years later.

**CRICKLEWOOD MPD** was in use for diesel locomotive servicing, when viewed on July 16th, 1967, as witnessed by the diesel fuel wagons in the yard.

*WT Stubbs Collection*

## 14B KENTISH TOWN

**Location**: The shed is east of the line, north of Kentish Town Station.(OS Map Ref; TQ 286856)

**Directions**: Turn right outside of Kentish Town (Northern Line) Station into Kentish Town Road, fork left into Highgate Road and turn left into an opening opposite Lady Somerset Road. A broad path leads from the end of this road to the shed.

**Closed**: April 1963

**Description**: Consisting of 3 brick built roundhouses.

**Post Closure History**: *Still Standing. In industrial use (1988)*

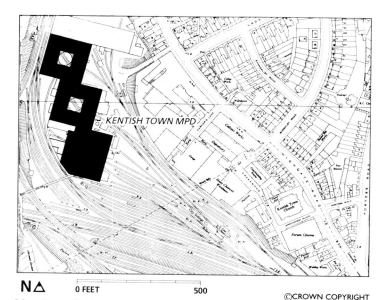

N△  0 FEET  500   ©CROWN COPYRIGHT

**Map Dated**: 1954

**Site Location**: North London. Adjacent to the west side of Highgate Road (B518).

**Track Status**: Kentish Town Station and lines are operational.

With all the locomotives tucked up indoors roundhouses rarely showed signs of the bustle and hurly burly of similarly sized straightsheds, **KENTISH TOWN MPD** was no exception when photographed in June 1958. *Photomatic*

## 34A KINGS CROSS

**Location**: The shed is in Kings Cross Goods Yard, north of Kings Cross Station. (OS Map Ref; TQ299838)

**Directions**: Turn sharp left outside the station along York Way, which runs parallel to the main line, and the Goods Yard entrance is on the left hand side. A road runs around the perimeter of the yard to the shed.

**Closed**: June 17th, 1963.

**Description**: A large shed complex consisting of a brick built 8TS through road shed, and a smaller brick built 7TS dead ended shed.

***Post Closure History***: *Demolished. Site partially occupied by a Freightliner Depot. It is anticipated that the whole site is to be incorporated within a major commercial redevelopment. (1989)*

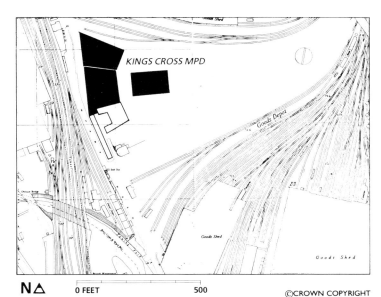

N△   0 FEET   500   ©CROWN COPYRIGHT

**Map Dated:** 1976 (Shed Superimposed)

**Site Location:** North London, on the west side of York Way (B513). *The most northerly building is the 'Met' Shed, adjoining the repair shop, with the Running Shed immediately east.*

A jam packed shed yard at **KINGS CROSS MPD**, complete with some of its famous collection of ex-LNER Pacific locomotives, on September 20th, 1959.

*WT Stubbs Collection*

## 34B HORNSEY

**Location**: The shed is on the east side of the Goods Yard, on the east side of Hornsey Station. (OS Map Ref; TQ310892)

**Directions**: Leave the station and turn right over the footbridge crossing the station. Turn right at the end into Hampden Road and the shed entrance is on the right hand side.

**Closed**: July 1961.

**Description**: A brick built 8TS dead ended shed.

***Post Closure History***: *Still Standing. In use as a stores depot, within the emu complex. (1988)*

N△   0 FEET   500   ©CROWN COPYRIGHT

**Map Dated:** 1955

**Site Location:** North London. On the south side of Turnpike Lane (A504) and west of Green Lanes (A105)

**Track Status:** Hornsey Station and line are operational.

No. 68891 heads a line of ex-LNER J50 0–6–0T engines at **HORNSEY MPD** in November 1959. By this time half of the shed area had been given over to diesel locomotives.

*Photomatic*

## 34E NEASDEN

**Location**: The shed is south of the line, west of Neasden (Bakerloo) Station. (OS Map Ref; TQ212849)

**Directions**: Turn right outside of the station along Neasden Lane and just before a railway bridge turn right along a cinder path. Proceed under another bridge and this path leads to the shed.

**Closed**: June 18th, 1962.

**Description**: A brick built 6TS dead ended shed.

**Post Closure History**: *Demolished during September 1967. Now site of Coal Depot. (1989)*

Ex-LMS locomotives dominate this view of **NEASDEN MPD** on September 20th, 1959.
*WT Stubbs Collection*

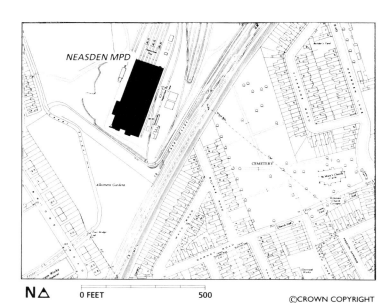

N△      0 FEET      500      ©CROWN COPYRIGHT

**Map Dated:** 1955

**Site Location:** North London. Between the North Circular Road (A406) and Neasden Lane (B453) and near Neasden Hospital.

**Track Status:** Lines are operational.

## 30A(s) WOOD STREET (WALTHAMSTOW)

**Location**: The shed is west of the line, north of Wood Street Station. (OS Map Ref; TQ385896)

**Directions**: Turn right outside of the station along Wood Street. Turn third right into Cuthbert Road and the shed entrance is at the end.

**Closed**: November 13th, 1960.

**Description**: A brick built 2TS through road shed.

**Post Closure History**: *Demolished. Now a Housing Estate*

With the electrification gantries fully installed **WOOD STREET (WALTHAMSTOW) MPD** was close to redundancy when photographed on April 2nd, 1960.
*Alec Swain*

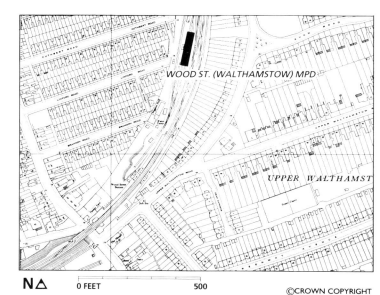

N△      0 FEET      500      ©CROWN COPYRIGHT

**Map Dated:** 1955

**Site Location:** North East London. South of Forest Road (B503) and east of Wood Street.

**Track Status:** Wood St.(Walthamstow) Station and line are operational. *The shed was demolished in December 1960.*

## 81C SOUTHALL

**Location**: The shed is in the fork of the Brentford and Paddington lines, east of Southall Station. (OS Map Ref; TQ133798)

**Directions**: Turn right outside of the station along South Road, turn right into Park Avenue and right over a footbridge over the railway lines. A flight of steps, in the centre of this bridge, leads to the shed.

**Closed**: January 3rd, 1966 (Steam).

**Description**: A brick built 8TS shed with 7 through roads.

*Post Closure History: In use as a diesel depot (SZ) until 1987. The shed was abandoned until September 18th, 1988 when the Great Western Preservation Group acquired the building and moved in its stock of locomotives, from Southall Warehouse, its previous headquarters. (1988)*

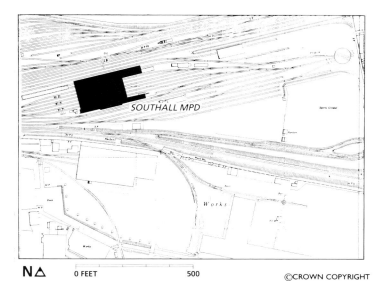

N△    0 FEET    500    ©CROWN COPYRIGHT

**Map Dated:** 1962

**Site Location:** West London. East of South Road (A3005) and south of Uxbridge Road (A4020)

**Track Status:** Southall Station and lines are operational.

*The shed closed for diesel locomotive purposes in November 1968 and was utilised for the servicing of dmus only until final closure.*

The DMUs and their servicing arrangements were firmly installed at **SOUTHALL MPD** as this photograph, taken on September 25th, 1963 clearly shows.

*WT Stubbs Collection*

## 1D DEVONS ROAD (BOW)

**Location**: The shed is on the east side of the Bow to Poplar line, south of Bow Station. (OS Map Ref; TQ377822)

**Directions**: Leave Bromley (by Bow) District Line Station by the Devons Road exit, turn left and continue into Brickfield Road. The shed entrance is a gate on the right hand side, opposite The Beehive Public House.

**Closed**: August 25th, 1958 (Steam). February 10th, 1964 (Totally)

**Description**: A brick built 10TS dead ended shed.

*Post Closure History: Following closure to steam it was converted for use as a diesel depot. It was demolished after total closure and is now the site of 'Devons Road Industrial Estate' (1988)*

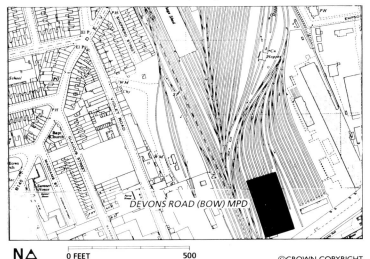

N△    0 FEET    500    ©CROWN COPYRIGHT

**Map Dated:** 1961

**Site Location:** East London. On the north bank of the Limehouse Cut, south of Devons Road (B140)

## SITE UTILISATIONS (4)

Depots built adjacently to busy railway stations virtually all succumbed to the same ignominious end - a station car park. This view, looking north, shows a former West Coast Main Line shed site doing good business in its new guise. **LEIGHTON BUZZARD MPD** was photographed in 1988.

*Paul Smith*

# PART FOUR
# SOUTH MIDLANDS

**BUCKINGHAMSHIRE    GLOUCESTERSHIRE    OXFORDSHIRE
HERTFORDSHIRE    BEDFORDSHIRE**

**TETBURY MPD** (Alec Swain)

# HERTFORDSHIRE

HITCHIN MPD
BUNTINGFORD MPD
BISHOPS STORTFORD MPD
WARE MPD
HERTFORD MPD
ST.ALBANS MPD
HATFIELD MPD
WATFORD MPD
RICKMANSWORTH MPD

## 14C ST.ALBANS

**Location**: The shed is east of the main line, south of St.Albans City Station. (OS Map Ref; TL156067)

**Directions**: Turn right outside of the station yard, over the bridge and turn first right into a rough road. A cinder path leads from this road to the shed.

**Closed**: January 11th, 1960.

**Description**: A brick built 2TS dead ended shed.

*Post Closure History: Demolished. The site is now in use as a Car Park.*

A derelict but totally intact **ST. ALBANS MPD** on July 17th, 1967, over 6 years after closure.
*WT Stubbs Collection*

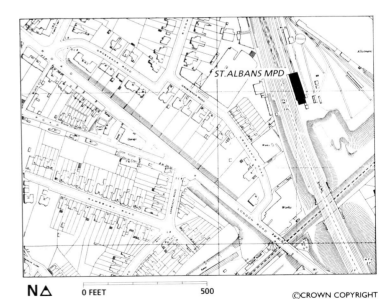

ST. ALBANS MPD

N△  0 FEET  500  ©CROWN COPYRIGHT

**Map Dated:** 1963
**Site Location:** In the south of the town, north of London Road (A5).
**Track Status:** St.Albans Station and line are operational.
*The shed was demolished in August 1968.*

## 30A(s) WARE

**Location**: The shed is on a small spur north of the line, east of Ware Station. (OS Map Ref; TL361139)

**Directions**: Turn left out of the station approach along Station Road, turn right at the end into Viaduct Road and the entrance to the Goods Yard is on the right hand side. The stabling point is within this yard.

**Closed**: January 3rd, 1966

**Description**: Consisting of a locomotive stand siding only, latterly used for stabling a diesel shunter.

**Post Closure History:** *Lines lifted (1989)*

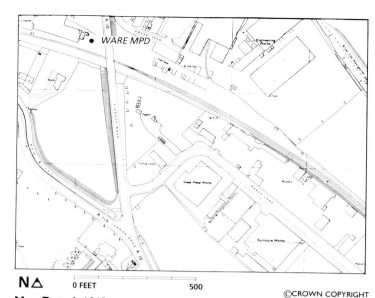

N△          0 FEET          500          ©CROWN COPYRIGHT

**Map Dated:** 1969

**Site Location:** In the town centre, adjacent to Viaduct Road (A10)

**Track Status:** Ware Station and line are operational. The Goods Yard has all lines lifted.

The diminutive stabling point at **WARE**, photographed from the adjacent road bridge on September 3rd, 1960.
*WT Stubbs Collection*

## 30C BISHOPS STORTFORD

**Location**: The shed consists of sidings on both sides of Bishops Stortford Station. (OS Map Ref; TL492209)

**Directions**: The shed office is adjacent to the eastern entrance to the station. Access to the sidings is from the ends of both platforms.

**Closed**: November 21st, 1960.

**Description**: Consisting of Engine Pits and water and coaling facilities. There are no shed buildings. Locomotives stand in sidings on both sides of the lines

**Post Closure History**: *Track Lifted. Sidings Overgrown. (1986)*

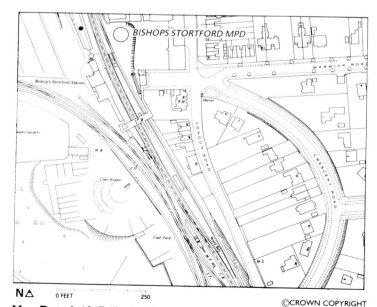

N△          0 FEET          250          ©CROWN COPYRIGHT

**Map Dated:** 1967 (Facility Superimposed)

**Site Location:** In the town centre, adjacent to the west side of London Road (A11).

**Track Status:** Bishops Stortford Station and lines are operational.

Britannia Class 4–6–2 No. 70003 *JOHN BUNYAN* drifts past the clutter of sidings that comprises **BISHOPS STORTFORD MPD** on one day in April 1958. The turntable is just visible to the left of the train, whilst a tank engine stands over the engine pit in the bay on the right.
*Photomatic*

## 34C HATFIELD

**Location**: The shed is on the west side of Hatfield Station.(OS Map Ref; TL232088)

**Directions**: Turn right outside the station, and right again into an alley. Proceed across the footbridge and the shed entrance is on the right hand side at the bottom of the steps.

**Closed**: January 2nd, 1961

**Description**: A brick built 2TS shed with one through road.

*Post Closure History*: *Demolished 1961.*

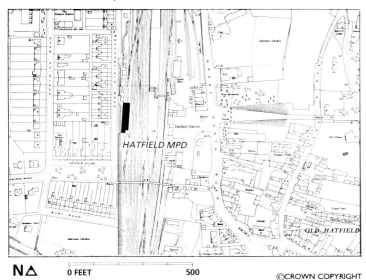

N△   0 FEET ──────── 500    ©CROWN COPYRIGHT

**Map Dated:** 1962

**Site Location:** In the east of the town, west of Great North Road (A1000) and immediately west of Beaconsfield Road.

**Track Status:** Hatfield Station and line are operational.

## 30B(s) BUNTINGFORD

**Location**: The shed is east of the line, at the south end of Buntingford Station. (OS Map Ref: TL364288)

**Directions**: Entrance to the shed is effected from the station platform.

**Closed**: June 15th, 1959

**Description**: Consisting of an Engine Pit, Water Tower and small Coaling Stage only. There are no Shed Buildings.

*Post Closure History*: *Now site of Housing Estate. (1988)*

The compact collection of facilities at **BUNTINGFORD MPD** on September 3rd, 1960.
*WT Stubbs Collection*

## 1C WATFORD JUNCTION

**Location**: The shed is on the east side of Watford Junction Station. (OS Map Ref; TQ114965)

**Directions**: Turn right outside of the station along a footpath running parallel to the main line, ascend the stairs into St.Albans Road, turn right over the bridge, and right again along a pathway. This leads to the shed.

**Closed**: March 29th, 1965.

**Description**: A brick built 6TS dead ended shed.

*Post Closure History*: *Demolished. Now site of Car Park.*

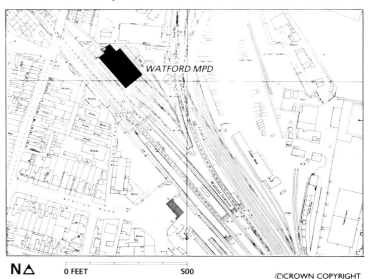

N△   0 FEET ──────── 500    ©CROWN COPYRIGHT

**Map Dated:** 1960

**Site Location:** In the east of the town, adjacent to the east side of St.Albans Road (A412).

**Track Status:** Watford Junction Station and lines are operational.

N△   0 FEET ──────── 500    ©CROWN COPYRIGHT

**Map Dated:** 1973 (Facility Superimposed)

**Site Location:** In the south of the town, adjacent to the west side of London Road (A10). From the map it will be observed that most of the facility is now buried under the front garden of No.9 Fairfield, and that the station building (immediately south west of The Shah public house) is still extant.

**Track Status:** Buntingford Station closed in 1964. Lines lifted.

## 34E(s) RICKMANSWORTH

**Location**: The shed is south of the line, west of Rickmansworth Station. (OS Map Ref; TO056946)

**Directions**: Entrance to the shed is effected from the station platform.

**Closed**: September 9th, 1961 (Line Electrification Date)

**Description**: Consisting of a mess room, two locomotive stand sidings, engine pit, coaling stage and water column. There were no shed buildings.

***Post Closure History***: *Lines Lifted. Site Unused. (1987)*

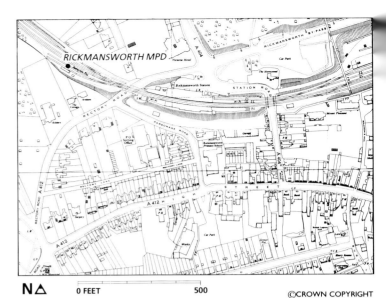

N△   0 FEET   500   ©CROWN COPYRIGHT

**Map Dated:** 1962

**Site Location:** On the east side of the town, adjacent to Rectory Road (A412)

**Track Status:** Rickmansworth Station and line are operational.

An indistinct, but nonetheless interesting view of **RICKMANSWORTH MPD**. The locomotive stand sidings still had steam facilities even though the electric rails were installed.     *Roger Griffiths Collection*

## 30B HERTFORD EAST

**Location**: The shed is north of the line, east of Hertford East Station. (OS Map Ref; TL334130)

**Directions**: Entrance to the shed is effected by means of a path from the station platform.

**Closed**: November 21st, 1960.

**Description**: A brick built 2TS shed, latterly with 1 through road.

***Post Closure History***: *Demolished 1961.*

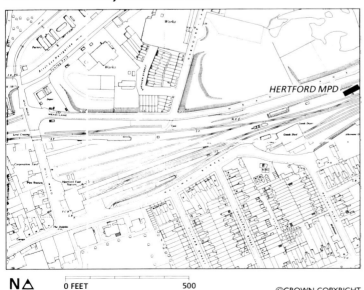

N△   0 FEET   500   ©CROWN COPYRIGHT

**Map Dated:** 1970 (Shed Superimposed)

**Site Location:** East of the town centre, adjacent to the south side of Mead Lane.

**Track Status:** Hertford East Station and line are operational.

## 34D HITCHIN

**Location**: The shed is east of the line, at the south end of Hitchin Station. (OS Map Ref; TL195297)

**Directions**: Cross the station yard, outside of the station, turn right under the railway bridge and a path leads up the embankment to the shed from the right hand side.

**Closed**: June 1961.

**Description**: A brick built 2TS dead ended shed.

***Post Closure History***: *Demolished, although two walls still remain.*

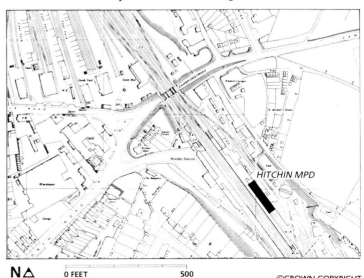

N△   0 FEET   500   ©CROWN COPYRIGHT

**Map Dated:** 1966

**Site Location:** In the east of the town, adjacent to the south side of Cambridge Road (A505).

**Track Status:** Hitchin Station and line are operational.

# BEDFORDSHIRE

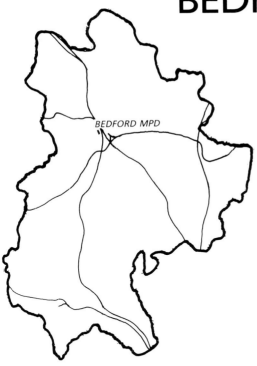

**Map Dated:** 1968 ▶
**Site Location:** South west of the town centre, adjacent to the south side of Ford End Road (A5141).
**Track Status:** Bedford Midland Road Station and lines are operational.

### 15D BEDFORD
**Location:** The shed is on the west side of the avoiding line, south of Bedford Midland Station. (OS Map Ref; SP042495)
**Directions:** Go straight ahead outside of Bedford Midland Station yard into Midland Road and after a few yards climb a flight of steps, on the right hand side. Turn right at the top and cross the long bridge. The shed entrance is at the bottom of the slope from this bridge, on the left hand side.
**Closed:** August 1963 (Steam)
**Description:** A brick built 4TS dead ended shed.
*Post Closure History: Still Standing (1988)*

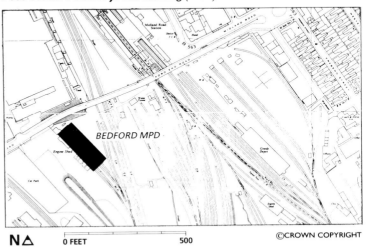

N △   0 FEET   500   ©CROWN COPYRIGHT

BR Standard Class 9F 2–10–0 No. 92028, fitted with Crosti Boiler, drifts past **BEDFORD MPD** on a down freight on September 4th, 1958.   *Ken Fairey*

# GLOUCESTERSHIRE

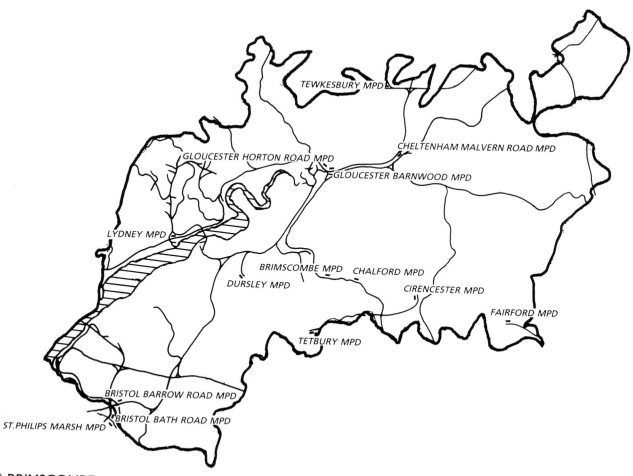

TEWKESBURY MPD

CHELTENHAM MALVERN ROAD MPD

GLOUCESTER HORTON ROAD MPD

GLOUCESTER BARNWOOD MPD

LYDNEY MPD

BRIMSCOMBE MPD    CHALFORD MPD

DURSLEY MPD    CIRENCESTER MPD

FAIRFORD MPD

TETBURY MPD

BRISTOL BARROW ROAD MPD

ST. PHILIPS MARSH MPD    BRISTOL BATH ROAD MPD

## 85B(s) BRIMSCOMBE

**Location**: The shed is north of the line, east of Brimscombe Station.(OS Map Ref; SO878022)

**Directions**: Entrance to the shed is effected from the station platform.

**Closed**: October 28th, 1963.

**Description**: A stone built 1TS dead ended shed.

*Post Closure History*: *Demolished. Site Unused.*

Ex-GWR 5100 Class 2–6–2T No. 5182 taking water at **BRIMSCOMBE MPD** on August 21st, 1960.

*WT Stubbs Collection*

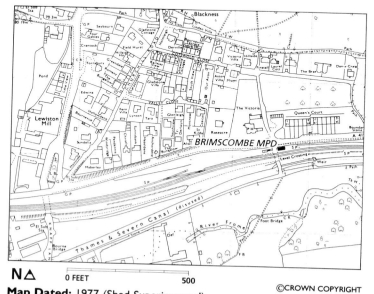

N△        0 FEET        500

©CROWN COPYRIGHT

**Map Dated:** 1977 (Shed Superimposed)

**Site Location:** In the south east of the town, immediately adjacent to the south side of London Road (A419).

**Track Status:** Brimscombe Station closed in 1964, the line is operational. *Although closed the shed remained in use until at least September 1964.*

## 85B(s) CHELTENHAM (MALVERN ROAD)

**Location**: The shed is on the north side of Cheltenham Spa Malvern Road station. (OS Map Ref; SO937224)

**Directions**: Turn left outside the station, along the approach road, and left again into Malvern Road. The shed entrance is a cinder path on the left hand side, just past a block of houses.

**Closed**: October 1963.

**Description**: A brick built 4TS dead ended shed.

**Post Closure History**: *Still standing and in use as a Timber Mill. (1988)*

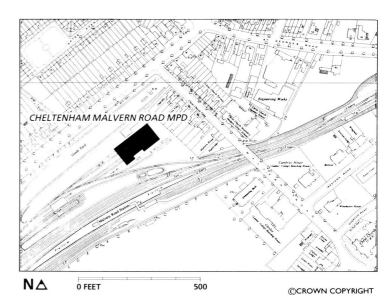

N△    0 FEET    500    ©CROWN COPYRIGHT

**Map Dated:** 1955

**Site Location:** In the north of the town, adjacent to the junction of Gloucester Road and Malvern Road.

**Track Status:** Malvern Road Station closed in 1966. Lines lifted.

**CHELTENHAM (MALVERN ROAD) MPD** on April 4th, 1958.

Bill Potter

## 22B(s) DURSLEY

**Location**: The shed is east of the line, north of Dursley Station.(OS Map Ref; ST756988)

**Directions**: Entrance to the shed is effected by following the line a short distance from the station platform.

**Closed**: September 10th, 1962.

**Description**: A brick built 1TS dead ended shed.

**Post Closure History**: *The building was used by RA Lister & Co. until at least 1972.*

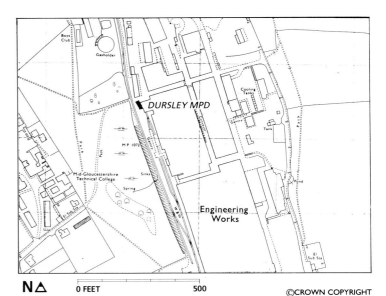

N△    0 FEET    500    ©CROWN COPYRIGHT

**Map Dated:** 1966

**Site Location:** In the north of the town, immediately east of Kings Hill Road and Mid-Gloucestershire Technical College.

**Track Status:** Dursley Station closed in 1962. Lines lifted.

Ex-LMS 0-6-0T No. 41748 taking water alongside **DURSLEY MPD** on June 8th, 1957

Bill Potter

## 85B GLOUCESTER HORTON ROAD

**Location**: The shed is at the north side of the junction of the Gloucester Central and Gloucester Eastgate to Cheltenham lines. (OS Map Ref; SO843183)

**Directions**: The entrance to the shed is opposite the entrance to GLOUCESTER (BARNWOOD) SHED, in Horton Road.

**Closed**: January 1st, 1966

**Description**: A brick built 10TS dead ended shed.

**Post Closure History**: *Partially demolished, in use as a diesel depot.*

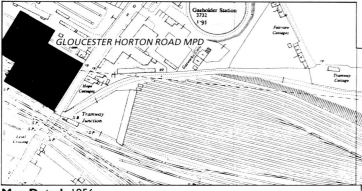

**Map Dated:** 1956

**Site Location:** In the north of the city, Horton Road leads southwards off Barnwood Road (A417).

**Track Status:** Gloucester Station and line are operational.

## 22B GLOUCESTER BARNWOOD

**Location**: The shed is on the north side of the Gloucester to Cheltenham lines, east of Gloucester Station. (OS Map Ref; SO847183)

**Directions**: Turn right outside the station and right into a subway leading under the station. Turn right into Great Western Road and right into Horton Road. A cinder path, on the left hand side just before the level crossing, and opposite the entrance to GLOUCESTER (HORTON ROAD), leads to the shed.

**Closed**: May 4th, 1964.

**Description**: A brick built roundhouse.

**Post Closure History**: *Demolished. Part of the site is RCE sidings, the rest is a ready-mixed concrete depot. (1988)*

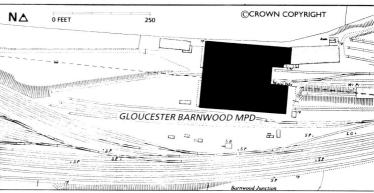

BR Class 9Fs feature strongly in this view of **GLOUCESTER HORTON ROAD MPD** taken on November 14th, 1965. *Bill Potter*

A single wagon occupies the shed yard at **GLOUCESTER BARNWOOD MPD** on September 27th, 1964, a few months after closure. *WT Stubbs Collection*

## 22A BRISTOL BARROW ROAD

**Location**: The shed is on the west side of the Fishponds line about 0.8 miles north of Temple Meads Station. (OS Map Ref; ST604730)

**Directions**: Go straight ahead across the yard outside the main exit from Temple Meads Station, turn left at the bottom of the hill into Temple Gate and first left into Cattle Market Road, passing under the station. Proceed into Feeder Road, turn left into Avon Street, pass under the railway bridge and turn right into Oxford Street. Continue into Days Road, turn left into Barrow Road and the shed entrance is on the left hand side of the railway bridge.

**Closed**: November 20th, 1965.

**Description**: A brick built roundhouse shed.

**Post Closure History**: *Demolished. Site Unused.*

**Map Dated:** 1951▶

**Site Location:** North east of city centre, Barrow Road leads southwards off Lawrence Hill (A420)

**Track Status:** The line is operational.

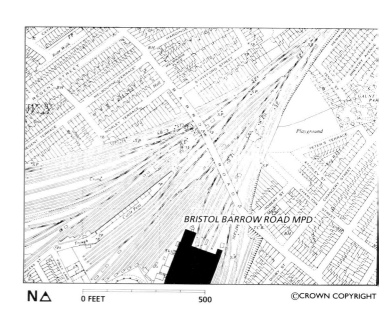

## 82B ST.PHILIPS MARSH

**Location**: The shed is south of the Bristol avoiding line, near the junction with the Taunton Line. (OS Map Ref; ST603720)

**Directions**: Follow the directions to BRISTOL BATH ROAD SHED, proceed past the entrance, turn left into an alley and continue over the bridge running alongside the line. Descend the steps and follow a road running parallel to, and beneath the line. A gate at the end of this road leads to the shed.

**Closed**: June 13th, 1964.

**Description**: A brick built double roundhouse shed.

*Post Closure History: Demolished. Now site of Wholesale Fruit and Vegetable Market, built in 1969.*

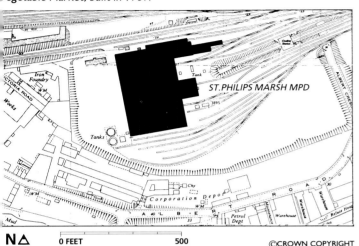

**N△**   0 FEET   500   ©CROWN COPYRIGHT

**Map Dated:** 1951

**Site Location:** South east of the city centre, north of Bath Road (A4)

**Track Status:** Lines operational

## 82A BRISTOL BATH ROAD

**Location**: The shed is on the east side of the line, south of Bristol Temple Meads Station. (OS Map Ref; ST599721)

**Directions**: Leave the station by the approach road and turn left along Temple Gate. Proceed along Bath Road and the shed entrance is on the left hand side, just past the railway bridge.

**Closed** (Steam); September 12th, 1960.

**Description**: A brick built 10TS dead ended shed

*Post Closure History: The buildings have been modified and partially demolished. Now a diesel depot (Code BR). (1988)*

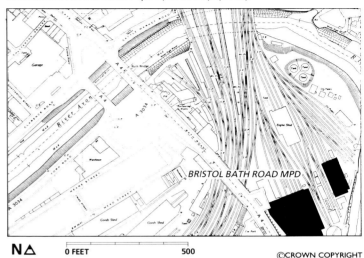

**N△**   0 FEET   500   ©CROWN COPYRIGHT

**Map Dated:** 1969

**Site Location:** South east of city centre. Immediately adjacent to east side of Bath Road (A4).

**Track Status:** Temple Meads Station and line are operational.

## 85B(s) TETBURY

**Location**: The shed is east of the line, at the north end of Tetbury Station. (OS Map Ref; ST883931)

**Directions**: Entrance to the shed is effected from the station platform.

**Closed**: April 1964

**Description**: A brick built 1TS dead ended shed.

*Post Closure History: Demolished. Site Unused. (1975)*

**TETBURY MPD** on June 21st, 1963.                    Alec Swain

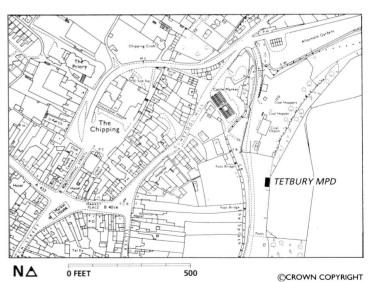

**N△**   0 FEET   500   ©CROWN COPYRIGHT

**Map Dated:** 1978 (Shed Superimposed)

**Site Location:** In the east of the town, on the east side of Gumstool Hill

**Track Status:** Tetbury Station closed in 1964 and the line was totally closed on April 4th, 1965. Lines lifted.

*The shed achieved universal fame as the basic design for Prototype Models Engine Shed.*

## 85B(s) CHALFORD

**Location**: The shed is north of the line, east of Chalford Station. (OS Map Ref; SO899024)

**Directions**: Entrance to the shed is effected from the station platform.

**Closed**: May 19th, 1951

**Description**: Consisting solely of an engine pit and single track. There are no shed buildings.

**Post Closure History**: Lines lifted. Site Unused.

A somewhat overgrown **CHALFORD MPD** finds use as a siding for goods wagons on August 21st, 1960, some 9 years after closure for locomotive purposes.

*WT Stubbs Collection*

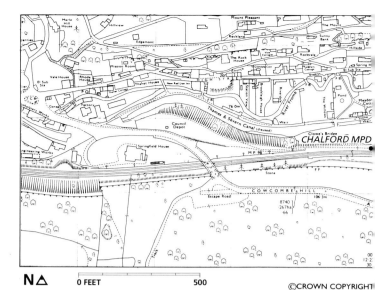

**Map Dated:** 1974

**Site Location:** South of the town, between the Thames and Severn Canal and Cowcombe Hill (A419)

**Track Status:** Chalford Station closed in 1964. Line operational.

## 85B(s) LYDNEY

**Location:** The shed is west of the Severn and Wye line, between Lydney Town and Lydney Junction Stations. (OS Map Ref; SO632021)

**Directions:** Turn right outside of Lydney Junction Station along Station Road, and the shed entrance is on the right.

**Closed:** March 2nd, 1964.

**Description:** A stone built 3TS dead ended shed.

**Post Closure History:** Demolished

One of the BR built 1600 Class 0–6–0PT locomotives No. 1630 stands in the shed yard at **LYDNEY MPD** on August 7th, 1957. *Bill Potter*

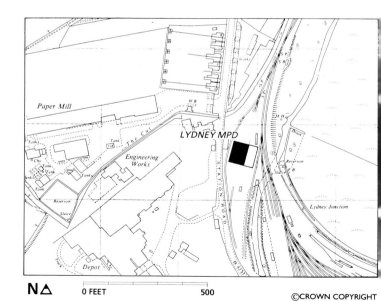

**Map Dated:** 1968 (Shed Superimposed)

**Site Location:** South of the town, immediately adjacent to the east side of Station Road (B4231)

**Track Status:** Lydney Junction and Town Stations closed in 1960. Lines lifted.

## 81F(s) FAIRFORD

**Location**: The shed is at the end of the branch, about 400 yards west of Fairford Station. (OS Map Ref; SP162008)

**Directions**: Entrance to the shed is effected from the station platform.

**Closed**: June 1962.

**Description**: A wooden built 1TS dead ended shed.

*Post Closure History: Demolished. Now site of Industrial Development. (1986)*

Ex-GWR 7400 Class 0—6—0PT No. 7404 nestles inside the timber built **FAIRFORD MPD** on August 21st, 1960.　　　　　*WT Stubbs Collection*

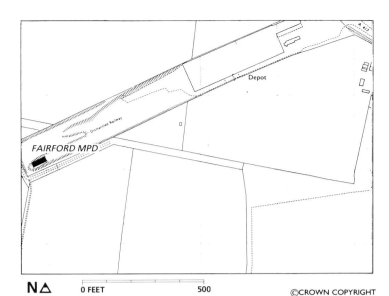

N△　　0 FEET　　　　500　　　　©CROWN COPYRIGHT

**Map Dated**: 1976 (Shed Superimposed)

**Site Location**: About half a mile east of the town, adjacent to the south side of the A417 road

**Track Status**: Fairford Station and line closed on June 18th, 1962. Lines lifted.

## 85B(s) CIRENCESTER

**Location**: The shed is south of Cirencester Town Station, west of the line. (OS Map Ref; SP022015)

**Directions**: Entrance to the shed is effected from the station platform.

**Closed**: April 1964.

**Description**: A wooden built 1TS dead ended shed.

*Post Closure History: The whole site is buried under a new road scheme.*

**CIRENCESTER MPD** photographed on August 21st, 1960.
　　　　　*WT Stubbs Collection*

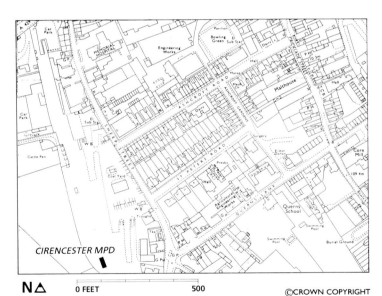

N△　　0 FEET　　　　500　　　　©CROWN COPYRIGHT

**Map Dated**: 1969 (Shed Superimposed)

**Site Location**: On the west side of the town, west of Sheep Street which runs southwards from Tetbury Road (A429)

**Track Status**: Cirencester Town Station closed in 1964. Lines lifted.

## 22B(s) TEWKESBURY

**Location:** The shed is on the north side of the Quay Branch, west of Tewkesbury Station. (OS Map Ref; SO895329)

**Directions:** Turn left outside of the station along Station Street and left at the end along Oldbury Road. Almost immediately turn left through some level crossing gates and this leads to the shed.

**Closed:** September 7th, 1962.

**Description:** A brick built 1TS dead ended shed.

*Post Closure History: Demolished in 1975, the site was redeveloped as dwellings in 1986.*

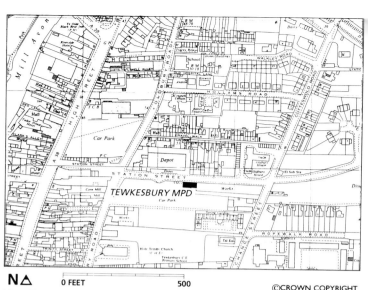

N△    0 FEET    500    ©CROWN COPYRIGHT

**Map Dated:** 1969 (Shed Superimposed)

**Site Location:** In the east of the town, immediately south of Station Street.

**Track Status:** Tewkesbury Station closed in 1961. Lines lifted.

A brace of ex-GWR 5700 Class 0–6–0PTs, Nos. 7756 and 7788 monopolise the small yard at **TEWKESBURY MPD** on March 11th, 1961.     *Bill Potter*

# FILM EXTRAS!

Two of the Motive Power Depots featured in this volume have, in British Railways days, found themselves involved in the production of British comedy films.

**BEDFORD MPD** *(Top)* was used to service the preserved ex-HR Jones Goods 4–6–0 No.103 during May 1964. The locomotive was employed during the filming of *Those Magnificent Men in their Flying Machines*, steaming up and down the now-defunct ex-MR Hitchin branch and assuming the role of a train in Northern France.     *Ken Fairey*

**HERTFORD EAST MPD** *(Bottom)* featured in the opening credits to the film *School for Scoundrels*, when the station masqueraded as "Yeovil". The film showed Ian Carmichael progressing from the train, through the station and station yard amongst an array of ex-LNER locomotives, and with the depot perfectly visible in the background.     *WT Stubbs Collection*

# OXFORDSHIRE

## 81D(s) HENLEY ON THAMES

**Location**: The shed is adjacent to the east side of Henley on Thames Station. (OS Map Ref; SU764823)

**Directions**: Entrance to the shed is effected from the station platform.

**Closed**: December 1958

**Description**; A wooden built 1TS dead ended shed.

*Post Closure History: The whole shed site is occupied by a small block of flats. (1988)*

A ramshackle **HENLEY ON THAMES MPD**, in private use on September 19th, 1963.
*WT Stubbs Collection*

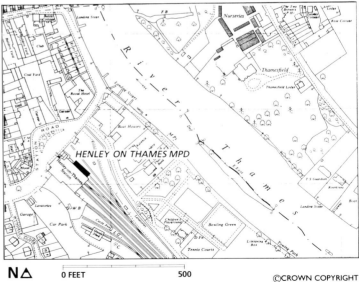

**Map Dated:** 1962

**Site Location:** South of the town centre and the A423 road, adjacent to the west bank of the River Thames.

**Track Status:** Henley Station and line are operational.

## 4A(s) OXFORD (LMS)

**Location**: The shed is on the east side of the ex-LNWR and ex-GWR lines, north of Oxford ex-LNWR and Oxford ex-GWR Stations. (OS Map Ref; SP505065)

**Directions**: Entrance to the shed is effected from the north end of the southbound platform of the ex-GWR Station.

**Closed**: December 3rd, 1950

**Description**: A brick built 2TS dead ended shed

**Post Closure History**: *Demolished, Site Unused.*

The long-closed **OXFORD (LMS) MPD** viewed from the ex-GWR shed yard on November 6th, 1960.
*WT Stubbs Collection*

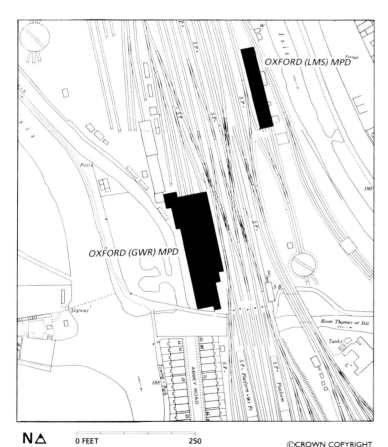

N△   0 FEET   250   ©CROWN COPYRIGHT

**Map Dated**: 1958

**Site Location**: In the west of the city, on the north side of Park End Street (A420)

**Track Status**: Oxford (GW) Station and line are operational. Oxford (LMS) Station closed in 1951. Lines lifted.

## 81F OXFORD (GWR)

**Location**: The shed is west of the line, north of Oxford (GWR) Station. (OS Map Ref; SP503067)

**Directions**: Turn right outside of the station into Cripley Road, proceed along Abbey Road and turn left into a cinder path at the end. Turn right over the canal bridge and right along the towpath, and the shed entrance is on the left, a short distance along.

**Closed**: January 3rd, 1966.

**Description**: A wooden built 4TS dead ended shed.

**Post Closure History**: *Demolished. Now site of a Diesel Stabling Point (Code OX). (1988)*

A somewhat smoky **OXFORD (GWR) MPD** shed yard on November 6th, 1960.
*WT Stubbs Collection*

## 81B(s) WATLINGTON

**Location**: The shed is east of the line, at the north end of Watlington Station. (OS Map Ref; SU696951)

**Directions**: Entrance to the shed is effected from the station platform

**Closed**: June 1957.

**Description**: Formerly a 1TS shed, destroyed by fire, and latterly consisting of a single track and Engine Pit only.

**Post Closure History**: *Lines lifted, but otherwise intact as recently as 1975.*

N△   0 FEET   500   ©CROWN COPYRIGHT

**Map Dated**: 1972 (Facility Superimposed)

**Site Location**: About one mile north of the town, adjacent to the east side of Watlington Road (B4009).

**Track Status**: Watlington Station closed in 1957 and the line closed totally on January 2nd, 1961. Lines lifted.

## 85A(s) KINGHAM

**Location**: The shed is in the fork of the Kingham to Kings Sutton and Worcester lines, north of Kingham Station. (OS Map Ref; SP256229)
**Directions**: Entrance to the shed is effected from the station platform.
**Closed**: December 1962.
**Description**: A brick built 1TS dead ended shed.
*Post Closure History*: *Demolished. Site Unused. (1987)*

BR Standard Class 2 2–6–0 No. 78001 stands at the simple coaling stage outside **KINGHAM MPD** on May 11th, 1957.                                              *Bill Potter*

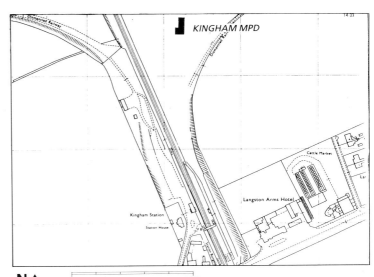

N△     0 FEET          500          ©CROWN COPYRIGHT

**Map Dated:** 1978 (Shed Superimposed)
**Site Location:** About one mile south of the town, adjacent to the north side of the B4450.
**Track Status:** Kingham Station and Worcester to Oxford line are operational. All other lines lifted.

## 84C BANBURY

**Location**: The shed is on the west side of the line, south of Banbury Station. (OS Map Ref; SP467398)
**Directions**: Turn left out of the station yard into a narrow road running parallel to the line. This leads to the shed, via a cinder path.
**Closed**: October 3rd, 1966.
**Description**: A brick built 4TS shed with 1 through road.
*Post Closure History*: *Demolished. Site Unused (1988)*

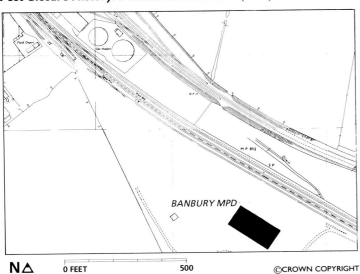

N△     0 FEET          500          ©CROWN COPYRIGHT

**Map Dated:** 1972 (Shed Superimposed)
**Site Location:** East of town centre, on the south side of the A422.
**Track Status:** Banbury Station and line are operational. The most northerly trackbed is the former LNWR line to Banbury Merton Street, closed in 1961.

# SHED PLATES

As discussed on Page 6 British Railways adopted the LMS *numeric-alpha* style of shed coding.

Cast iron shed plates had originated on the Midland Railway at about the turn of the century, but it was not until the LMS reorganisation in 1935 that the now-familiar coding was utilised throughout its network, and this became the basis of the full BR Shed Coding List. By using this method each depot could be identified, not only as to its operating area but also as to its status within that area, basic information that was not readily ascertained from the initial/abbreviations style of coding in use on the other networks.

The LMS shed plates, more often than not, used a serif style of lettering, BR standardised on Gill Medium for theirs, the oval plate measuring 7½ in x 4½ in, but as can be discerned from the 2 examples illustrated the actual style utilised appeared to depend upon the whim of the foundry pattern makers engaged in their production.

During the transition from steam to diesel, shed plates found themselves attached to the bodysides of diesel locomotives, usually painted in the livery colour. This practice petered out to be replaced much later by self-adhesive vinyl stickers displaying the 'new' diesel codes, a system that had been discarded in 1948, initial letters of the depot!

# BUCKINGHAMSHIRE

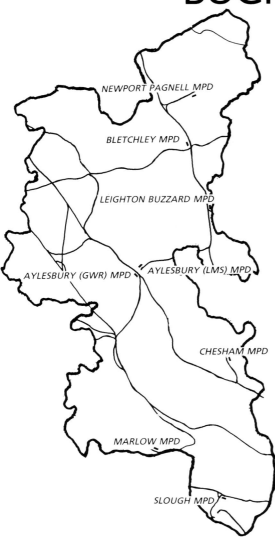

**Map Dated:** 1972 (Shed Superimposed)▶
**Site Location:** On the east side of the town centre, adjacent to the junction of Lock Road and Station Road.
**Track Status:** Marlow Station closed in 1967 and was relocated further east along the line. Lines lifted.

## 81B(s) MARLOW
**Location**: The shed is north of the line, at the east end of Marlow Station. (OS Map Ref; SU855866)
**Directions**: Entrance to the shed is effected from the station platform.
**Closed**: July 1962
**Description**: A brick built 1TS dead ended shed.
*Post Closure History: Demolished. The whole site is now occupied by a Housing Estate. (1989)*

The diminutive **MARLOW MPD** on September 19th, 1963.   *WT Stubbs Collection*

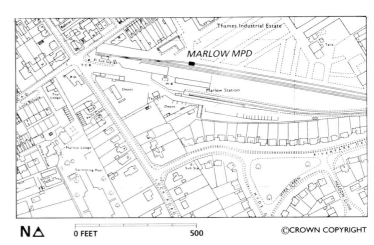

N△   0 FEET   500   ©CROWN COPYRIGHT

## 34E(s) CHESHAM
**Location**: The shed is at the south end of Chesham Station. (OS Map Ref; SP961015)
**Directions**: Entrance to the shed is effected from the station platform.
**Closed**: September 11th, 1960.(Line Electrification Date)
**Description**: Probably unique. Consisting of an engine pit on the running line adjacent to the platform and water tower, the locomotive stabling on the end of the train at weekends. A coaling stage is on the east side of the Goods Yard, at the north end of the station.
*Post Closure History: The pit has been filled in and electrified rails installed. The Goods Yard has been rebuilt as a Coal Depot. (1988)*

©CROWN COPYRIGHT

**Map Dated:** 1971▶
**Site Location:** On the east side of the town centre, Station Road runs eastwards from High Street (A416).
**Track Status:** Chesham Station and line are operational.

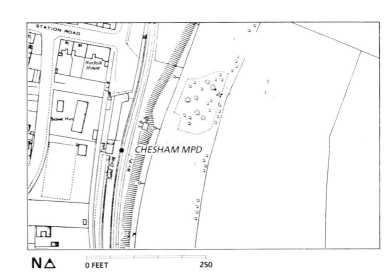

N△   0 FEET   250

## 4A(s) AYLESBURY (LNWR)

**Location**; The shed is in the Goods Yard, west of the line and north of Aylesbury (High Street) Station. (OS Map Ref; SP824138)

**Directions**; Entrance to the shed is effected from the station platform.

**Closed**; January 31st, 1953.

**Description**; A brick built 1TS through road shed.

*Post Closure History; The station site is now occupied by an office block, whilst the remainder, including the shed site, is utilised for Car Parking. (1988)*

**AYLESBURY (LNWR) MPD** in pre-war days.                    *W.A.Camwell*

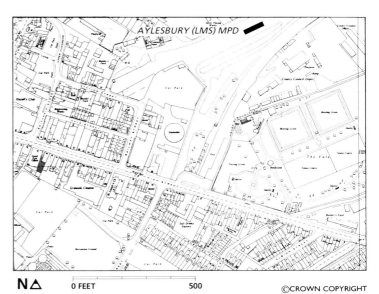

N△        0 FEET                    500            ©CROWN COPYRIGHT

**Map Dated:** 1966 (Shed Superimposed)

**Site Location:** North east of town centre, at the end of Railway Street which runs northwards from High Street.

**Track Status:** Aylesbury High Street Station closed in 1953. Lines lifted.

## 81B(s) AYLESBURY (GC)

**Location**; The shed is adjacent to the former GC/Met Station on the west side of the line. (OS Map Ref; SP818134)

**Directions**; Entrance to the shed is effected from the north end of the down platform.

**Closed**; June 16th, 1962

**Description**; A brick built 2TS shed, with 1 through-road.

*Post Closure History; Demolished, The shed site is part of industrial premises. (1970)*

A pretty full **AYLESBURY (GC) MPD** on May 29th, 1959.        *Alec Swain*

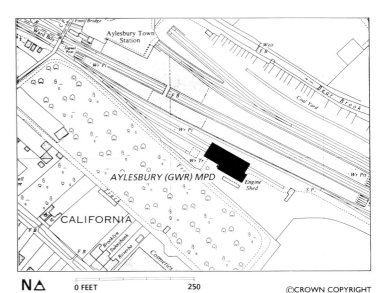

N△        0 FEET                    250            ©CROWN COPYRIGHT

**Map Dated:** 1966

**Site Location:** South of town centre, adjacent to ring road.

**Track Status:** Aylesbury Station and line are operational.

## 4A BLETCHLEY

**Location**: The shed is on the west side of the West Coast Main Line, just north of the station. (OS Map Ref; SP868338)
**Directions**: The shed entrance is in the station yard.
**Closed**: July 15th, 1965.
**Description**: A brick built 6TS shed with 1 through road.
***Post Closure History***: *Now site of Station Car Park. Parts of the original perimeter walls are still in situ. (1988)*

A typical ex-LMS shed building, this one is **BLETCHLEY MPD**, photographed on September 18th, 1963. *WT Stubbs Collection*

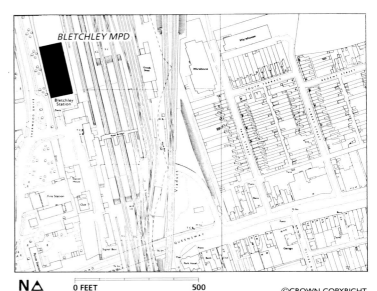

**Map Dated:** 1971 (Shed Superimposed)
**Site Location:** West of the town centre, on the north side of Queensway.
**Track Status:** Bletchley Station and lines are operational.
*The shed was totally demolished in 1966.*

## 4A(s) NEWPORT PAGNELL

**Location**: The shed is east of the line, south of Newport Pagnell Station. (OS Map Ref; SP872437)
**Directions**: Entrance to the shed is effected from the station yard.
**Closed**: June 13th, 1955.
**Description**: A wooden built 1TS dead ended shed.
***Post Closure History***: *Demolished, September 1957.*

A pre-war view of the timber-built **NEWPORT PAGNELL MPD**. *W.A.Camwell*

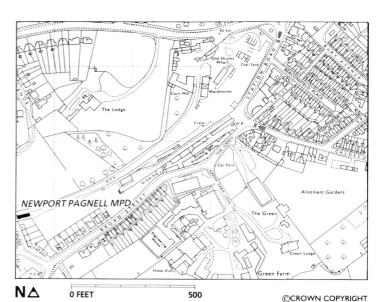

**Map Dated:** 1971 (Shed Superimposed)
**Site Location:** South west of the town centre, adjacent to the west side of Station Road (B488).
**Track Status:** Newport Pagnell Station closed in 1964. Lines lifted. Most of the trackbed is in use as a walkway.

## 4A(s) LEIGHTON BUZZARD

**Location**: The shed is east of the line, south of Leighton Buzzard Station. (OS Map Ref; SP911248)

**Directions**: The shed entrance is a gate in the station yard.

**Closed**: November 5th, 1962.

**Description**: A brick built 2TS through road shed.

*Post Closure History: Demolished, the shed site is now part of the Station Car Park.*

**LEIGHTON BUZZARD MPD**, typically housing ex-LNWR locomotives in October 1954.
*John Edgington*

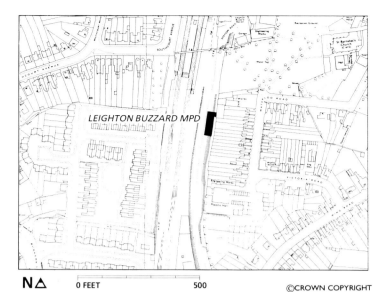

N△   0 FEET   500   ©CROWN COPYRIGHT

**Map Dated:** 1972 (Shed Superimposed)

**Site Location:** West of the town centre, south of the B4032 road.

**Track Status:** Leighton Buzzard Station and line are operational.
*The shed was demolished in August 1963.*

## 81B SLOUGH

**Location**: The shed is south of the main line, adjacent to the junction of the Windsor line, west of Slough Station. (OS Map Ref; SU974801)

**Directions**: Turn right outside of the station into the approach road, continue into the main road and the shed entrance is on the opposite side of this road.

**Closed**: June 1st, 1964

**Description**: A brick built 5TS shed with 4 through roads.

*Post Closure History: Demolished. The site was in the process of commercial development during 1989.*

**SLOUGH MPD**, complete with lean-to extension on September 25th, 1963.
*WT Stubbs Collection*

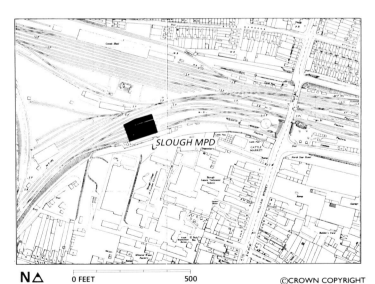

N△   0 FEET   500   ©CROWN COPYRIGHT

**Map Dated:** 1956

**Site Location:** West of the town centre, on the west side of William Street (A332)

**Track Status:** Slough Station and lines are operational.
*The shed was demolished in 1972.*

# INDEX